India for Indians

India for Indians

CHITTA RANJAN DAS

GYAN

Published by

GYAN

Gyan Publishing House
5, Ansari Road
Daryaganj, New Delhi-110002
Phone: 011-47034999, 9811692060
E-mail: books@gyanbooks.com

Distribution Network
gyanbooks.com
India, USA, Canada, UK, Australia, France

ISBN: 978-81-212-8816-3 (PB)
First Published, 1917

2nd Impression 2023

Printed at: Gyan Press, Delhi.

INDIA FOR INDIANS
Author: Chitta Ranjan Dasa

C. R. Das.

India for Indians

BY

CHITTA RANJAN DAS

WITH FOREWORD BY

BABU MOTILAL GHOSE

(*Editor, A. B. Patrika.*)

GANESH & CO., MADRAS.

CONTENTS

OM

FOREWORD

When the Publishers asked me for a Foreword to this small volume of Speeches by Mr. C. R. Das, I readily acceded to their request, both from personal and public considerations.

Personally I have known Mr. Chitta Ranjan Das from the days of his youth. His father, the late Babu Bhuban Mohan Das was a friend of mine. Bhuban Mohan was a well-known Attorney of the Calcutta High Court. For sometime he was connected also with Bengalee journalism. As editor, first, of the *Brahmo Public Opinion*, and subsequently of the *Bengal Public Opinion*, he made a very high position for himself among Bengalee journalists. His style was very simple, and he spoke with a directness that was rather rare in our more successful English weeklies of those days. Babu Bhuban Mohan was a sincere patriot, and though like good many English educated Bengalees of his generation, he threw himself heart and soul into the Brahmo Samaj Movement, in his personal life and more particularly in his dealings with his Hindu relatives, he belonged to the old Hindu type, and spent whatever he earned,—and he earned a lot—for the support of his poorer relatives. Indeed he spent upon them more than his finances allowed and consequently got involved in heavy liabilities that forced him, during the closing years of his professional life, to take refuge in the Insolvency Court.

Chitta Ranjan was educated, I think, in the London Missionary College, Bhowanipore; and subsequently in the Presidency College, Calcutta whence he took his B.A. degree and went to England to qualify himself for the Indian Civil Service. I do not remember if he actually competed for the I.C.S. He joined the Inns of Court and was called to the Bar in the early Nineties.

Chitta Ranjan gave considerable promise of exceptional literary and oratorical gifts even when he was a student in the Presidency College, Calcutta. While in England he made some political speeches, in connection I think, with the Electioneering Campaign of Mr. Dadabhai Naoroji, and some of those speeches were very favourably noticed by the English and the Indian Press.

Upon his return home, and within a short time of his joining the Calcutta Bar, he took upon himself the responsibility of all his father's debts; an act that forced him at the very commencement of his professional career, to join his father in seeking the protection of the Insolvency Court. It was not only a filial duty, but a point of honour, with Chitta

Ranjan to share this indignity with his father. He was very seriously handicapped, both in his professional and in his public life, by this insolvency. But for it, Chitta Ranjan would have long ago publicly thrown himself into all our political and patriotic movements and won the position of leadership to which he was entitled by his capacity and his devoted love for his country.

Though his exceptional abilities were universally recognised, from the very beginning of his career as a member of our High Court Bar, he could not secure adequate scope for them for a good many years; pecuniary struggles forced him to abandon the chances of a successful practice in the High Court for the mufassal practice which is more profitable to a junior Barrister.

The celeberated Conspiracy Case against Srijut Aravinda Ghosh, in which he appeared as Aravinda's Counsel pushed Chitta Ranjan into the fore front of the Calcutta Bar. Great was the sacrifice that he made in undertaking this defence. For more than six months he was engaged in this case, and the fee that he received was not sufficient to meet even all his household expenses during these months; and he had to incur a large debt for this purpose. The acquittal of Aravinda at once raised the reputation of his Counsel, and from the very day that Chitta Ranjan came back to take up the broken threads of his High Court practice, he found himself on the high road to both fame and wealth. This reminds me of the saying of Sree Bhagavan in the Geeta—that the doer of good never comes to any grief.

As soon as he found his position in this profession secure, Chitta Ranjan's first thought was to remove the stain of insolvency from his father's name and his own and he started to pay off every pie of those old debts. This is the first time, as Mr. Justice Fletcher declared, that a discharged insolvent publicly accepted his old liabilities and applied for a formal discharge of his insolvency. This act of unusual fidelity to his financial obligations, at once raised Chitta Ranjan Das to the position of a great moral hero.

Having secured his discharge from his insolvency, Chitta Ranjan found himself free to freely and openly join all our public activities; and as the new National Life in Bengal, denied free scope and outlet in politics by the restrictive legislations of Lord Minto, had commenced to seek and find expression in a variety of literary organisations. Chitta Ranjan threw himself into this Nationalist Movement, and soon found, himself among its great leaders. In 1915 he started a new Bengalee Monthly, the *Narayana*, which secured for its contributors some of the highest literateurs of Bengal, including Maha-Mahopadhyaya Hara Prasad Sastri who has an European reputation, and Babu Bepin Chandra Pal. Chitta Ranjan's entry into Bengalee literature dates from 1894 or 1895 when he published a volume of Bengalee lyrics, called *Malancha* which introduced a new element of freedom and realism into our modern lyrical literature. During the last two years, two more volumes of Lyrics have been published by him. The last annual Literary Conference of Bengal, in recognition of his literary services, nominated Chitta Ranjan as the President of its Literary Section while the political leaders of the Province offered him an equal recognition by asking him to preside over our last Provincial Conference.

The speeches collected and published in this volume are the latest pronouncements of Mr. C. R. Das upon some of the pressing political problems before us. They have already attracted considerable notice from the Anglo-Indian press, and the virulance of these criticisms are themselves a *prima facie* proof of their worth and importance. I will not try any criticism of these here. The reader will be able to judge of their value himself. Students of current political literature in this country will find in these a freshness of ideas and a freedom of treatment which are so much needed just now for the formation of a sound and healthy public opinion among us.

Mr. C. R. Das, though yet young, is already an esteemed and prominent leader of Bengal. His patriotism is genuine ; his abilities are unquestioned. Self-seeking is not in his line. He tries to serve his motherland according to his light, not for his own aggrandisement but for her welfare alone. He is above official frowns or favours—his independence is fearless. He is not a pushing man yet his talent has pushed him forward to a foremost place both in his profession and the political field. He earns a good deal of money but perhaps spends more. His charities are many though the general public know very little of them. He has a fine heart, which is ever ready to help a fellow in distress, even at a considerable personal sacrifice. If he does not convert himself into a mere money-making machine like many worthy members of his profession, he is bound to prove a tower of strength to the national cause. He is a Home Ruler and a democrat of democrats, every inch of him. To me he is specially dear, as he is a devotee of Sri Krishna and Sri Gauranga. As his father's friend, I have the privilege of passing benediction on him. May God grant him a long and healthy life and enable him to devote it unselfishly to the service of man and his maker.

AMRITA BAZAR
PATRIKA OFFICE, CALCUTTA,
12*th November*, 1917.

MOTI LAL GHOSH.

INDIA FOR INDIANS

HINDU MAHOMEDAN MASS MEETING

On the 7th October 1917, an enthusiastic Mass Meeting was held at Calcutta, when Mr. C. R. Das as Chairman of the meeting spoke as follows :—

Gentlemen, —When this morning Mr. Akran Khan called upon me to request me to preside over this meeting, I felt it was a call of duty to which I must respond. My heart is filled with gladness to find that on this platform and at this meeting Hindus and Mahomedans of Calcutta have met together to fight their common battle. Indeed in the days of the Swadeshi movement in 1905, I knew—and my friend Mr. Bipin Chandra Pal will bear me out—we knew that the day was not far distant when the Hindus and the Mahomedans will fight shoulder to shoulder in the cause of their country. I did not then know that the time was so near. While I must give expression to this feeling I feel at the same time, a sense of deep loss. I refer to the death of my friend Mr. Rasul. How I wish he had been here to-day to fight this battle with us shoulder to shoulder, how I wish his presence had animated us to-day. Gentlemen, on the morning of the day that he died, I felt this loss but I feel it overwhelmingly to-day in this vast assembly. There is no man in Bengal, Hindu or Mahomedan who was more respected by the whole Bengalee race. There is no man in Bengal who fought so much, who exerted himself to such an extent to bring about the union between Hindus and Mussalmans of this country and if I may be permitted to say so, he was almost the pioneer amongst Mahomedans, the first who felt that the interest of the Hindus and the interest of the Mahomedans is the same in spite of religious differences. Gentlemen, we have met to-day to protest against the policy of internment and to ask for the release of the gentlemen who have been interned. Who are the persons who are specially mentioned in your notice? I am sure you will agree with me that these are names which are respected by Mahomedans and Hindus alike. The name of Mahomed Ali is a household word in India. I had the honour of his friendship, We met together often when he was in Calcutta and I can tell you that there is no more sincere and ardent patriot in the whole of this country than Mr. Mahomed Ali. Mr. Shaukat Ali, I do not know personally but I have heard accounts of him from many of my friends which show that this gentleman is an unselfish patriot. This gentleman had been engaged in the work of union between Hindus and Mahomedans all over India and certainly such a man is worthy of esteem and honour. The last name is that of

Sham Sunder Chakravarty. I have had personal acquaintance with him. I have been bound with him by ties of friendship and I can assure you, gentlemen, that Sham Sunder Chakravarty is incapable of having done anything which deserved his internment. I have given you the honoured names which are mentioned in this notice. But over and above these few names I can tell you there is hardly a home in East Bengal from which one or more persons have not been interned. Every home in East Bengal is filled with sadness to-day, because these people have been snatched away from their homes and imprisoned without trial or without proof. I protest on your behalf against this policy of internment. I say this policy is un-British, is opposed to all the time honoured traditions upon which the British Empire is based. It is opposed to all rules of common sense and prudence and uprightness and the sooner this policy is abrogated the better for the peace and prosperity of the empire.

Gentlemen, at a time when the British Government in its wisdom has declared its policy that Home Rule in some shape or other must be granted to this country that some sort of responsible Government is necessary for the foundation and preservation of the empire; at a time when His Excellency the Viceroy has advised us to preserve an atmosphere of calmness; I ask, is it wise to detain these men against popular opinion, against the universal desire of the Indian people. And why should they be detained? May we not tell those who are responsible? You detain them under an Act which has been characterised by the highest authorities in England and in this country to be illegal and ultra vires. You have detained these men and other persons on political considerations which are outside the purview of the Defence of India act under which you claim to detain them. Gentlemen, I wish to read to you a passage from the judgment of one of the greatest judges in England—I may say that the Act in England is similar to the Act under which these gentlemen have been snatched away from society and kept imprisoned, This learned Judge, Lord Shaw than whom a nobler judge there is not in the whole of England says —You remember, gentlemen, in England persons of German origin have been sought to be detained in this way and His Lordship says:—" But does the principle, or does it not, embrace a power not over liberty alone but also over life?" His Lordship says that if by the stroke of a pen you can take away the liberty of a man, does it not also follow that by the stroke of a pen you can take away his life also? His Lordship goes on to say:—

" If the public safety and defence warrant the Government under the Act to incarcerate a citizen, without trial, do they stop at that, or do they warrant his execution without trial? If there is a power to lock up a person of hostile origin and associations because the Government judges that course to be for public safety and defence, why, on the same principle and in exercise of the same power, may he not be shot out of hand? I put the point to the learned Attorney-General, and obtained from him no further answer than that the graver result seemed to be perfectly logical. I think it is. The cases are by no means hard to figure in which a Government in a time of unrest, and moved by a sense of duty, existed, it may be, by a gust of popular fury"

in this case the Anglo-Indian fury

"might issue a regulation applying, as here, to persons of hostile origin or association, saying, Let such danger really be ended and done with; let such suspects be shot.' The defence would be, I humbly think, exactly that principle, and no other, on which the Judgments of the Courts below are founded—namely, that during the war this power to issue regulations is so vast that it covers all acts which, though they subvert the ordinary fundamental and constitutional rights, are in the Government's view directed towards the general aim of public safety or defence."

"Under this the Government becomes a Committee of Public Safety. But its powers as such are far more arbitrary than those as of the most famous Committee of Public Safety known to history."

This is what one of the greatest of English Judges has said. Now, gentlemen, we next come to these particular cases. Mr. Mahomed Ali, as you all know—and if I have said more of him, you will pardon me, because he was a friend of mine,—he was asked to give an undertaking. He gave it but he said : "Subject to the injunctions of my religion." They are all the facts which have appeared in the letter of his mother whom judging from her letter, we all hold in deep veneration ? Judging from that letter it seems to me that Mr. Mahomed Ali was not released because he would not give an unconditional undertaking, because he did not say. "What ever the injunctions of my religion may be I give an undertaking, the undertaking which you want." Well, gentlemen, I pause for one moment and I ask you to consider according to what right or what principle does the Government of this country or any government in the world, ask a man to give up his opinion and his religion ? Ought he to submit to it ? Is it not his duty to say at once, "I do not care what you do but it is my religion, I stand on it and here in this sphere I am a free man, You may hold my body imprisoned but my soul is in the hands of God." Now gentlemen, exactly, that illustration was given by this great judge in his judgment. His Lordship goes on to say :—

"No far-fetched illustrations are needed ; for, My Lords, there is something which may and does move the actions of men often far more than origin or association, and that is religion. Under its influence men may cherish belief which are very disconcerting to the Government of the day, and hold opinion which the Government may consider dangerous to the safety of the realm. And so, if the principle of this construction of the statute be sound, to what a strange pass have we come! A regulation may issue against Roman Catholics—all, or, say, in the South of Ireland, or against Jews—all, or, say in the East of London,—they may lose their liberty without a trial. During the war that entire chapter of the removal of Catholic and Jewish disabilities which has made the toleration of British famous through the world may be removed not because her Parliament has expressly said so, but by the stroke of the pen of a Secretary of State. Vested with this power of proscription, and permitted to enter the sphere of opinion and belief, they, who alone can judge as to public safety and defence, may reckon a political creed their special care, and if that creed be socialism, pacifism, republicanism, the persons holding such creeds may be regulated out of the way, although never deed was done or word uttered by them that could be charged as a crime. The inmost citadel of our liberties would be thus attacked. For, as Sir Erskine May observes, this is "the greatest of all our liberties—liberty of opinion."

Gentlemen, is life worth living if we have not that liberty of opinion? You may differ from me, I may differ from you—you must be allowed to hold your own opinion, I must be allowed to hold mine. Members of the Civil Service may hold one opinion, I may hold another opinion. His Excellency the Viceroy may hold another opinion. His Majesty the King Emperor personally may hold one opinion and I may hold the contrary opinion—but is opinion a crime ? Has it ever been a crime in the history of civilization ? We hoped that the dark ages have gone but it seems that it still lingers. Now, apart from the opinion of this great judge, I rely,—I venture to think I have got the right to rely—upon the gracious Proclamation of 1858. Let me quote to you, gentlemen, the passage which has been often quoted and which we regard as our Magna Charta. It says this ;—

"Firmly relying ourselves on the truth of Christianity and acknowledging with gratitude the solace of religion, we disclaim alike the right and the desire to impose our convictions on any of our subjects. We declare it to be our royal will and pleasure that none be in anywise favoured, none molested or disquieted, by reason of their religious faith or observances, but that all shall alike enjoy the equal and impartial protection of the law; and we do strictly charge and enjoin all those who may be in authority under us that they abstain from all interference with the religious belief or worship of any of our subjects on pain of our highest displeasure."

Gentlemen, I venture to think, that the Government, His Excellency the Viceroy or the Members of Council whoever may be responsible for it, has absolutely no right to demand an undertaking which in any way goes against the dictates of his religion. I hold in my hands the Magna Charta,

I hold in my hands the very words used by Queen Victoria Empress of India, viz., "all those we charge and strictly enjoin, who may be in authority" and in this case the Council here is in authority,-" that they abstain from all interference with the religious belief or worship of any of our subjects on pain of our highest displeasure." His Excellency should know and the Council should know that by this act they are going against the Proclamation of 1858, according to which they would incur the displeasure of His Majesty the King. It is not we who are against the King, it is not we who are going against the principles upon which this Empire is based. It is those who Snatch away our liberty without just cause, without trial. Now, gentlemen, all these considerations might have been placed before the Government—I am sure the Government would have listened and done justice—but there is a difficulty in our way.

The difficulty is the European Association. We are used to the tricks of the European Association. In the days of the Ilbert Bill Agitation, we saw what the Anglo-Indians can do. But then, public opinion had hardly been born in this country. Today, again when the British Government has recognised the policy of self-Government we hear the same uproar. These people who come here to make money, who come here penniless and when they retire, take away thousands and thousands—these people pretend to talk in the name of India when they say that these gentlemen, these honoured gentlemen should not be released because they knew that if they are released, they will strengthen the party which seeks Self-Government, because they know that when Mr. Mahomed Ali comes out, when Babu Sham Sunder Chakravarty comes out, they will fight shoulder to shoulder for the cause of Self-Government in this country. And if Self-Government is granted what about the policy of these merchants? If Self-Government is granted the authority of Magistrates and Collectors in every district will be lessened—and then what would happen to these gentlemen who write letters to Collectors saying,—my dear so and so, will you see this done and will you see that done? It is a notorious fact in this country—and I have heard complaints from many Indian Merchants engaged in the coal trade—that they cannot get waggons at a time when English merchants are fully supplied with waggons. These are the advantages which they get by this country being ruled not by the people of this country but by a bureaucracy. That really is the reason of this Anglo-Indian agitation.

I must refer to the speeches made by these knights of Anglo-India against the interests of this country and against the policy of Self-Government. I will first of all refer to the foolish speech of Arden Wood. This gentleman is reported to have said: "If racial feeling is to be dominant in Indian politics the time will come, when we, the British will either have to leave India or reconquer it." Now, gentlemen, it is difficult to take this speech seriously. They may leave India if they find it unprofitable to stay in India. They may stay in India if they find it profitable to do so but the tall talk of reconquering India is a comical statement. It reminds me of the bravery of the valiant Pistol and Corporal Nymph. If this gentleman does not know, he ought to know that India was never conquered. India was won by love and won by promise of good government. India was never conquered and God willing, it will never be conquered for all time to come. India will impress her ideal, her civilization, and her culture upon the whole world. The work has commenced to-day. It will go on increasing till the world will listen to the message of India.

Some of the other speakers made very angry speeches. One gentleman is reported to have said that if there is a government by the people and for the people then there will be no security for life and "prosperity." Mark the word prosperity. I do not know whether the printer's devil is responsible for this but if he is, this devil has got a perfect knowledge of the internal affairs. The apprehension of this speaker is that if there is Self-government, there will be no security or prosperity. Whose prosperity may we ask? Is it the prosperity of India, is it the prosperity of the teeming millions of our country or is it the prosperity of Sir Archy Birkmyre? Whose prosperity? If the granting of Home Rule to this country means the poverty of Sir Archy Birkmyre, let it be so, but still

Self-government must be granted. India does not live for Sir Archy Birkmyre or the petty traders who come here and rob us of our money. India lives for herself—she has lived for herself for centuries and she will live in herself and for herself for all time to come. There is another statement made by this angry speaker, which takes my breath away. He says that this agitation of the European Association is to assert the rights of the British in India. The rights of the British in India! The little-minded traders who at a time when the Government enjoins a calm atmosphere, hold a meeting and proceed straight away to denounce the whole country; and abuse the people and all the ideals for which they fight and in which they live and move and have their being—these men claim the right to represent the British. The British indeed! When His Majesty's ministers say that there should be Home Rule, there should be Self-Government, that the people of this country should be granted equal partnership with the people of England in the Empire, who are these traders who claim to represent British interest in India? Gentlemen, I will not take you through the many comical statements made by this entertaining band of players, Jones-Birkmyre Company. They are used to many tricks. I will refer to some of the 'Statesman' newspaper, which used to pose as the Friend of India at one time. I think it has given up all that pretence now. This "Statesman" came out one day with a furious article on the Extremists of Bengal and praised the Moderates and the next day it said that there did not seem to be any difference between the Extremists and the Moderates. Well, the reason for that is quite clear. There is in fact, no difference. This distinction was invented by the "Statesman" newspaper some years ago. We can frankly tell the Anglo-Indian community that there are no Extremists among us, no Moderates. The Hindus and Mahomedans of Bengal are all Nationalists—they are neither Extremists nor Moderates. I may tell you who are the Extremists. It is those Anglo-Indian Agitators who are the worst Extremists. You talk of a calm atmosphere! Who broke that calm? It is you Anglo-Indian Agitators. It is Sir Hugh Bray, it is the Lieutenant-Governor of the Punjab, it is the speakers who spoke at the meeting of the European Association. These people broke the calm. I ask them to consider the position and beware. The days of the Ilbert Bill agitation have gone by. These are the days of rising Democracy in this country. We will no longer tolerate that sort of vapourings, that kind of abuse. If, in spite of that, they persist in their wicked agitation, we shall soon know how to deal with them. We are fighting in the best interests of the Empire, we are fighting for the ideal expressed by the King's ministers; we are fighting for carrying out that very policy which has been declared in England by His Majesty's ministers, and by His Excellency the Viceroy in this country. If you dare stand against that, we will know how to deal with you. Be assured, we Indians do not deny your legitimate share whatever may be the extent of that share in the Government of this country. We know what you mean when you say that Self-government is no good, because Self-government would be against the interests of the teeming millions of India. We know the hollowness of that hypocricy. But we can tell these gentlemen, so far as I am concerned, at any rate, I am perfectly clear,—that we shall accept no Self-government, no Home Rule unless it recognises and includes within it the teeming millions of India. When I ask for Home Rule, for Self-Government, I am not asking for another bureaucracy, another oligarchy in the place of the bureaucracy that there is at present. In my opinion, bureaucracy is bureaucracy, be that bureaucracy of Englishman or of Anglo-Indians or of Indians. We want no bureaucracy, we want Home Rule, we want Self-government by the people and for the people. We want Self-government in which every individual of this country, be he the poorest ryot or the richest zemindar—will have his legitimate share. Every individual must have some voice. We want Home Rule, broad based on the will of the people of India. Now, gentlemen, this is our objective. Do they still say or can they, in reason, say, that we are not asking Home Rule on behalf and in the interest of the teeming millions of India? If they say we have got no right to ask for it in their interest, my answer is we have a thousand times greater right to ask for them than you who never know them or care for them. India has always been tolerant towards those people, whatever their religious creed or faith may be, who have made India their Home—every one of them is my brother and I embrace him with open arms. The history of India has made it abundantly clear. We have the Parsis in India. They adopted India as their home and to-day we embrace them as our brothers. We have had hosts of Mahomedan invaders who came to this country as conquerors but they made this country their home and to-day we embrace them with open arms. If these Anglo-Indians want to make India their home, let them do so and we will work hand in hand with them in the interest of the Indian Empire. But if they come here to make money and all their interest is how best to make it, I say they are no friends of India, they have got no right to call themselves Indians, they have got no legitimate right to oppose the granting of self-good to the people of India. I say to them. " Come here if you wsnt. Make money if you can. Go away in peace if you want to do so."

I said that our difficulty is, the mischievous working of the European association. Let us be united, gentlemen. Let us assist the Government against this selfish and unreal agitation. I feel sure the victory is ours.

PUBLIC MEETING—MYMENSINGH

A large meeting of the people of Mymensingh was held in October 1917, at the Surjakanta Hall, under the presidency of Babu Anathbandhu Guha to formulate a scheme of responsible Government for India, when Mr. C. R. Das addressed as follows :—

Mr. Chairman, and gentlemen—I thank you heartily for calling upon me to address you to-night. This is my first visit to Mymensingh. Before I arrived here, I really did not know that I had so many friends amongst you. My friend Mr. Guha has referred to my unselfish activities. I am sure I do not deserve that praise. But this I will claim for myself that whenever the interest of the country required my services, I have never lagged behind. I might not have always adopted the right course—I might have been wrong, every one of us is often wrong but I have always honestly tried to place the interest of the country above all considerations. With me work for my country is not imitation of European politics. It is part of my religion. It is part and parcel of all the idealism of my life. I find in the conception of my country the expression also of divinity. With me nationality is no mere political conception borrowed from the philosophy of the west. With me a nation has to grow because a nation must grow. God's universe teems with varieties of life. Every nation is one unit of such life. Every nation must grow, to the evolution of life. The nation to which I belong must also grow, only we must help in its growth. I value this principle of nationality as I value the principle of morality and religion. The service of country and nationality is service of humanity. Service of humanity is worship of God.

BENGAL HAS A MESSAGE TO DELIVER

To-night I wish to say a few words to you about the present political situation in our country, Do not imagine gentlemen, that your political situation is detached from other matters which belong to our country. Political activity is part and parcel of your culture; it is the practice of your patriotism; it is the expression of your religion. I never believe in watertight compartments of human culture. There are people of this country, who try to divide the whole field of human life into so many compartments or divisions. With them politics is one thing, religion, education—these things have nothing to do with politics. With them religion is a different branch altogether. Neither politics nor education has anything to do with it. They forget that human soul is one, they forget that the individuality of human beings is one complex whole covering many activities. As the individual soul is one, so the national soul is one. I do not desire to deal with the political situation of to-day in any narrow spirit or in a spirit which is borrowed from the politics of Europe,—much as I venerate European culture, much as I love and much as I acknowledge my indebtedness to the education which I had in Europe, I cannot forget that Bengal stands for something higher than that. I cannot forget that our nationality must not rest content with borrowing things from European politics—and I repeat what I said elsewhere, that Bengal has a message to give to the world. When you will find that infant nationality has grown and we have developed according to our light, our country will deliver that message and the world will listen.

PREDOMINANT NOTE IN THE POLITICAL SITUATION

Now, gentlemen, what is the predominant note in the political situation of to-day. I refer the many attempts which are being made to introduce in this country some kind of Self-government. Some people call it Self-government, others call it Home Rule, others again Swaraj—but we need not quarrel with words, they all mean the same thing. I would much rather you should give your attention to the thing itself than the name with which you want to call that thing. Now, what is it which is necessary in the interest of our race—not only in the interest of our race (but in the interest of the world at large)—for no race can have its self-interest fulfilled in the highest degree without at the same time contributing to the interest of the empire and of the human race. So I ask you to consider what is necessary for you to have by way of Self-government. It is abundantly clear that the highest authorities in England have come to the conclusion —our politicians and many other persons who have devoted their time and energy to the cause of the country have also come to the conclusion—that we must have some form of Government which may be described as Government by the people and for the people.

WHAT OUR POLITICS CONSISTS IN

Now gentlemen, I desire to point out one thing clearly here. It has been said by Anglo-Indian newspapers and Anglo-Indian agitators that our politics consist in abusing the Government. Well I deny that charge in toto. Our politics consists in this that we want some kind of Government which may be described as responsible Government according to the principles of constitutional law. We want some sort of Government in which the Government officials will be responsible to the people whom they govern. We have no quarrel with individuals. If a civilian official does some wrong in some place we feel we have to criticise his actions. But my objection will not be met by replacing the whole of the Civil Service by Bengalees. My quarrel is not with individuals, my quarrel is with the system—it is an evil system. It might have been necessary at one time. It has done its work and is no longer necessary. It hampers our growth at the present moment—anything which stands against our growing nationality, I have no hesitation in describing that as an evil. The time has come when this system should be cast away as a 'creed outworn,'

WHAT KIND OF GOVERNMENT WE WANT

Gentlemen, if you have once made up your mind that you want some kind of Government which will be responsible to the people, the next point to consider will be, what kind of Government is it that you want. We cannot forget that we live in the midst of an empire, the largest and the most glorious empire in the history of the human race. We cannot forget that our interests are bound up intimately with the interest of England. We cannot forget that our interests are also bound up with the interests of Australia and South Africa. All of us live and grow under the sway of the same Empire. If you consider the geographical magnitude of this Empire, the different races, the different creeds, the different cultures, the different religions which this empire represents, you will find that here is a glorious opportunity for federating so many human races, with so many distinct interests, distinct nationalities, different cultures, different religions and in that way for contributing to the ultimate federation of the whole human race. That is the philosophy of nationalism to-day. Therefore first of all, we must get a government which will be autonomous in so far as it will be government by the people.and for the people, The different provincial governments are to be connected together by some sort of central government and then again that central government is to be connected up with the different parts of this vast empire. That is the sort of Government for which the time has come for which to make a definite scheme.

THE RENUNCIATION OF POLICY

The proclamation of 1858, impliedly promised some such free autonomous representative government. Years rolled by, we passed through many changes, we had many different promises on different occasions, but these promises had never been redeemed. The other day, His Majesty the King-Emperor came to this country and from his lips, we had the message of hope. Though we have been disappointed over and over again, the time has come when these promises must be redeemed. In connection with the political situation of the present moment, I ask you to consider first the statement of the Secretary of State for India, which was published on the 20th August last (1917). I invite your particular attention to the words of that statement. I will read out to you certain portions which are significant of what is to come.

" The policy of His Majesty's Government etc., etc., is that of increasing the association of Indians in every branch of administration and the gradual development of self-governing institutions with a view to the progressive realization of responsible government in India, as an integral part of the British Empire etc., etc."

I draw your particular attention to the words "Progressive realization of responsible government in India, as an integral part of the British Empire." That is the ideal which the Secretary of State has sketched out. What is the deduction from this? What is it that we have got to hope for from this statement? It is this : that there will be several representative institutions and that these institutions will be responsible institutions and that these institutions will form the Government of India, which will be an integral part of the British Empire. Now, what does that mean? It means that there should be autonomous governments in every province that these provincial governments are to be responsible and autonomous, that is to say, responsible not to the Government of India, not to anything which is above them, but to the people, the electors who would elect the representatives to these autonomous legislative bodies. That is the doctrine of responsible self-government as it is understood in politics and in constitutional law. Now, therefore, you get these provincial governments which are responsible to the people, i.e. the members being elected by the people and you get these autonomous governments connected with the Government of India and again the Government of India connected with the Empire.

How that connection will be served has been described by certain political thinkers in England but I do not desire to deal with it because before it is declared as the policy of Government, we have no right to take those utterances as part of any statement by the Government. Having sketched out this ideal, the Secretary of State goes on to say; "They have decided that substantial steps in this direction should be taken as soon as possible etc., etc."

Therefore, gentlemen, you get two things perfectly distinct in this statement and I appeal to you that you should not lose sight of these two, viz. the ideal of responsible government which will be representative in the highest sense of the word and which will be connected with the empire and secondly, some steps should be taken immediately in that direction. That is the declaration of policy made by His Majesty's Government. We have, therefore, a right to expect that some definite steps will be taken soon towards the practical attainment of that ideal.

THE VICEROY ON SELF-GOVERNMENT

The next thing to which I wish to refer is the speech of His Excellency the Viceroy, delivered on the 5th of September. I will only refer to that part of it which deals with this ideal of self-government. His Excellency says :—

" I now turn to the third task, viz., constitutional reforms. At the very first Executive Council, which I held as Viceroy and Governor-General,' I propounded two questions to my Council : (1) What is the goal of British Rule in India? (2) What are the steps on the road to that goal? We came to the conclusion which, I trust most Hon. Members will agree, was inevitable, that the endowment of British India, as an integral part of the British Empire, with self-government was the goal of British Rule, and His Majesty's Government have not put forward in precise terms their policy, which we may say that we as the Government of India regard in substance as practically indistinguishable from that which we put forward, etc., etc."

Having said what the goal is, His Excellency proceeds to say that the first road to that goal is in the domain of local self-government, village, rural, town or municipal.

The second road is in the domain of more responsible employment of Indians under the Government. Referring to the third, His Excellency says :—

"We come now to our third road, which lay in the domain of Legislative Councils. As Hon. Members will readily appreciate, there is no subject on which so much difference of opinion exists, and with regard to which greater need is required for careful investigation and sober decision. I may say frankly that we, as the Government of India, recognise fully that an advance must be made on this road simultaneously with the advances on the other two, etc., etc."

I draw your attention to this. We, therefore, have got the right to hope that not only will this work of local self-government commence but simultaneously, along with that, work in the other two domains must also commence, His Excellency says:—

"And His Majesty's Government, in connection with the goal which they have outlined in their announcement have decided that substantial steps in the direction of the goal they define should be taken as soon as possible."

I say, therefore, gentlemen, that we have got a right to expect that in the near future some substantial steps should be taken for granting to the people of this country that government which is responsible, which is representative and which is an integral part of the British Empire.

HOW DIFFICULTIES BEGAN

After these declarations were made, difficulties began. On the one hand, it filled us with hope that many of us, I must confess, did not examine this statement minutely and critically and had only a vague impression as to what was going to be done and were unduly suspicious, but on the whole, it has made us hope for the realization of that which we have been fighting for, for the last 50 years, On the other hand, it gave rise to despair in other people. I would ask you to mark the dates. The statement of the Secretary of State was made on the 20th of August. On the 13th of September the memorable pronouncement was made by His Excellency the Viceroy. On the 20th

September, Sir Hugh Bray and Mr. Hogg spoke in the Indian Legislative Council; and they at once made it clear that it was nonsense to think of any kind of Self-government so far as India is concerned. I ask you to note that fact because I shall ask you to consider what followed, in the light of that interesting event which took place on the 20th September. I am referring to the speeches made by Sir Hugh Bray and Mr. Hogg. Now, Sir Hugh Bray, apart from criticising the political activities of the people of this country—I will not retaliate by abuse for abuse—made it perfectly clear by saying this: "It is not we who wanted a change in the method of Government," So, Sir Hugh Bray does not want a change in the method of Government. The European Association, 6 days after, declared that they did not want a change in the method of Government in this country.

IS IT A WILD INFERENCE?

Is it a wild inference to draw from these two significant events that these people did not want a change in the method of Government in this country, because they know the present system of Government is the most profitable to them? If any one draws that inference, is he to be characterised as a violent speaker? I say the dates and the speeches speak for themselves. It is idle to say afterwards we were not against changes, we wanted our interest to be safeguarded." The fact is they did not want a change and why should they? If I had been an Anglo-Indian merchant, I should not have wanted a change. They say that they have sunk capital in this country. I do not know the exact extent of that capital. My impression is—I speak from my impression and I am subject to correction, but I think I am right—that for whatever capital they invested, they have taken out a great deal more in the shape of profits, But granting that they have sunk capital in this country, what right does it give them to dictate to the people of this country that the method of this particular Government is not to be changed. British capital has been invested in America, France and Germany. Does any British Merchant ever dream that they have got the right to dictate to the American, French, or German Government about the method of their particular Government? Why is it that the sinking of capital should have such a different effect on the soil of this country? The reason is perfectly clear. In America, they would not stand such nonsense, in France they will be asked to keep quiet. But it is only in this country that these merchants who have sunk capital—I am assuming that they have and that it still remains unrealised—can put forward the claim that the Government of this country should be run in their interest and not in the interest of the people of India. They see the absurdity of their position and because they see the utter absurdity of this illogical and extravagant claim which they make in furtherance of their self-interest they have to say that they are the real representatives of India. They say: "We are speaking not only on our behalf but on behalf of the teeming millions of this country. You are professional agitators," I do not understand what they mean by "professional agitators"—nobody pays me or Mr. Surendra Nath Banerjea or any of my friends for making speeches. However, what they mean is this: that the speakers belong to a particular profession (?) I happen to belong to law. Many of my friends who have to make speeches belong to the medical profession or some other profession. But these speakers of the European Association also belong to some profession or trade. Sir Archy Birkmyre has also his trade to ply, the other merchants I suppose make their profits, Mr. Jones of the "Statesman" gets his wages—and even the fire-eator of the Lamartinaire College must draw his pay. Mr. Pugh I do not think forgets to send in his bills of costs. That is not what they mean. They have got to find out some ground of abuse. Therefore they say "Oh those professional agitators, these wicked agitators, do not listen to them for one single moment. The teeming millions of this country do not want them." No, gentlemen, our countrymen do not want us. They want Mr. Jones of the "Statesman" and the other celebrities who exhibited their eloquence at that meeting! These worthies next proceed to demonstrate the utter absurdity of any idea of self-government for us.

THE CHARGE OF ILLITERACY.

Mr. Jones in his speech says that out of a total of 315 millions of people in this country only a very few know how to read and write. I take it that he asks us to infer from that people who do not know how to read and write are worthless—they have got no conscience of their own they do not know what is good and what is bad—they cannot choose between Mr. Jones and Mr. Surendra Nath Banerjea. Well, I deny that proposition. I do not know what it is in Europe but so far as the teeming millions of our country are concerned, I have very often come across men who are called illiterate, but I can assure you that great many of them are shrewd men of business. They are certainly competent to judge as to who could look after their interest better whether it is Sir Archy Birkmyre or any one of us. They are certainly in a position to judge that. But if they are illiterate, may we ask why have they remained so? What has the Government done, if at the close of a hundred and fifty years, so many in this country have remained illiterate, and in such a state that they cannot choose their own representatives? That itself is the surest condemnation of the present method of Government. It has got to be changed and I can assure you if some kind of self-government is granted to us in the near future within the next twenty years there will not be one single illiterate man in this country. I throw out this challenge : let them put us in that position, give us power to work out our own good and I am sure that before many years are over the people in this country will be better than people of most countries. The illiteracy of our people is one of the strongest grounds upon which we put our claim for Home Rule. We say that we are not being allowed to develop. We say that our infant nationality is being choked. We are the inheritors of a great culture. We are the stewards of a spirituality which must be presented to the world. We must rekindle that fire. That which is dormant must be brought to life and light. Self-government alone can do that. Gentlemen, be he European or Indian, who stands for self-government in this country stands for Humanity and God. Our Anglo-Indian friends have this glorious opportunity. The other day in Calcutta I criticised their speeches. To-day I wish to refer to some of the statements made by Mr. Jones of " Statesman."

FRIENDLY ANTICS OF THE "FRIEND OF INDIA."

You remember, gentlemen, we had some differences in the Reception Committee. We have made them up. I do not wish in the least degree to refer to any of these disputes, but these are disputes which must occur in every healthy community, in every political organization, which is not absolutely lifeless. As soon as these disputes occurred, the "Statesman" was in high glee. What did it say? "Oh the extremists, you have been found out; oh, the good moderates, do not mix with the extremists, we will embrace you. Don't you make that mistake." Articles were written, crying down the extremists and heaping abuse upon them. If any Indian speaker had used half those expressions, he would at once have been denounced by the "Stateman" as a wild agitator. But the "Statesman" is not wild, it is very tame and in that tame way, it tried to accentuate the differences between the two parties. Our disputes were settled as they must be settled. If they had not been, both parties would have accepted the decision of the All-India Congress Committee. Directly the disputes were settled, the "Statesman" thought of the stories of Alphonso and it tried to be jocular. In one of the stories, the "Statesman" said, it is said that kids do not eat up wolves but it is the wolves who eat up kids; and the wolves of the extremists have eaten up the kids of the moderates. However, the revelation came upon Mr. Jones not after many years but in the course of a few days that there were no Moderates in India. I entirely agree with him; only I wish to add a rider that there are no Extremists either. We are all Nationalists.

After a few days the question of the internment of Mr. Mahomed Ali arose and I had the honour of presiding over a meeting in Calcutta of both Hindus and Mahomedans to protest against the internments. The next day, the "Statesman" published long accounts of Bakr-Id riots and said that Hindus and Mahomedans in this country could never unite. That is the policy of the "Statesman." Do you believe that the "Statesman" newspaper ever thought that there was any possible distinction between the people whom it characterised as Extremists and those whom it characterised as Moderates? Does the "Statesman" not know that the interests of Mahomedans and the interests of Hindus are identical? of course, it knows but it chooses not to say so because it has got its own interests to serve. I wish to call some gems from Mr. Jone's speech.

GEMS FROM MR. JONES' SPEECH

He says: "Because I am satisfied that in this country the struggle will be very hard, possibly fruitless"—oh, the pathos!—it breaks my heart—"and that our real course of action lies in bringing the cant home to the people of England and impostures with which they have been stuffed." Cant and imposture with which the British people have been stuffed—that is the general proposition I quote from Mr. Jones:

"The next imposture, the next abuse of political terms is connected with these words Legislative Councils. There are Legislative Councils in the Colonies which are really and truly Legislative Assemblies corresponding to our Parliament."

Nobody has any doubt about that!

"Now, a Legislative Council in India is a very different thing."

Exactly so! That is our grievance, we complain that our Legislative Councils are shams. They are without power, without responsibility. But let us see how he makes that out to be an imposture;

"But the trick played is to confuse the two and to make out to the British people that a Legislative Council in India is just such a representative body as one of these Colonial Parliaments."

MR. JONES' LOGIC

Have you ever heard anything like that? Yet this is said by Mr. Jones. He says that we Indians have said in England that our Legislative Councils are exactly like those in the Colonies. Is not it too ridiculous for words? We say that our Legislative Councils are shams because they are not representative. We ask for such a grant of Home Rule that our Legislative Councils may be like those in Australia. But Mr. Jones says that we have deceived the English people by saying that our Legislative Councils are truly representative bodies. Does he think that he was doing some conjuring trick? Well, that is the sort of imposture with which he fed his audience. I will give you one other sample and finish with Mr. Jones. You have read those speeches and noticed that when the name of the Secretary of State was mentioned by one of the speakers the audience hissed aloud. If any speech could bring the

Government into discredit and contempt, it was the speech of Mr. Jones. The people who become violently immoderate in speech and sentiment when their selfish interests are attacked are the people who lecture us to be moderate in our expressions. I ask you to say if I am not right in calling these agitators as extremists. I said elsewhere there are no moderates or extremists among us, but the real extremists are those people who by their actions and by their words have betrayed the Government of this country and also the people of this country.

OUR ATTITUDE LOYAL THROUGHOUT.

Our whole attitude on the question of self-government is to hold to the banner of the moirs. Our attitude has been loyal throughout and as I read out to you the statements of the Secretary of State and the Viceroy you have found that our demands are based on the words and the spirit of those statements. We are for the empire, they are for selfish interests of their own. We are for a great ideal, they are for their money. That is the difference between the Anglo-Indian agitators and ourselves. Well, gentlemen, do not be troubled by these agitators. Let them go on in their way. They ought to realise that the days of the Ilbert Bill agitation are dead and gone and buried for ever. They have no right to dictate anything to the Government.

A WORD TO ANGLO-INDIAN EXTREMISTS

The Government of the country has openly declared its policy and the people of this country are in sympathy with that policy; they will try to assist the Government in carrying out that scheme. And if these Anglo-Indian Extremists should come in the way, they should be told once for all that India is not their home, India is our home—our fathers have lived here for thousands of years. The dust of this country is sacred to us. Every incident of its history is part of our Scripture. Who are you who have come here to make profits, who are you to stand between us and the Government?

UNDER THE BANNER OF THE EMPIRE

I say again the message of hope which His Majesty the King-Emperor gave us is about to be redeemed. The banner of the empire is uplifted. Let us close our ranks; let us be united. Let us put forward a definite, and reasonable and sufficient scheme. Let us not be timid. Let us not be foolhardy. Let us fight this battle for the honour of this country and for the glory of the empire.

A GREAT MEETING AT DACCA

A meeting of the citizens of Dacca was held in the spacious room of the Bar Library on the 11th October 1917, Babu Ananda Chandra Ray, Dacca, presided, when Mr. C. R. Das spoke as follows :—

Mr. Chairman, and gentlemen,—I thank you very much for calling upon me to address you to-night on the question, which of all questions is agitating the mind of all of our countrymen to-day. Whatever the Anglo-Indians may say, I believe, I am speaking the truth when I say that there is hardly an educated man in the country who is not to-day thinking of self-Government. And I say further that every educated man in this country has a right to think of Self-Government. If you consider the history of the public events for the last five years, you cannot but oome to the conclusion that the time has come when the educated community of this country, taking such assistance from their uneducated brethren as they can, must think out clearly and rationally as to what form of Self-Government they might expect and they insist upon.

HIS MAJESTY'S MESSAGE OF HOPE

Gentlemen, I begin with the King-Emperor's Message of Hope which His Majesty personally delivered to this country before he left the shores of India and his voice still rings in our ears. We did not know then what that message was but this we know that the great question which had been agitating the mind of our countrymen for many years had also left some impression on the minds of our rulers. Gentlemen, after that, many proposals have been put forward for the introduction of some kind of Home Rule or Self-Government in this country.

MR. MONTAGU'S STATEMENT

But it was only the other day, I believe on the 20th of August, that the statement of the Secretary of State was published. I do not know, gentlemen, whether you have read that message clearly and carefully. You will find in that statement an indication that the message of Hope which was delivered by His Majesty personally is about to be fulfilled, You will remember what the Secretary of State says in that statement that some kind of responsible government is to be granted to this country. Gentlemen, I will not deal with that in detail, as I had dealt with it yesterday at Mymensingh.

THE VICEROY'S SPEECH

But I cannot help repeating one thing before you *viz.*, that precisely the same messsage, the same indication is to be found in the speech of His Excellency the Viceroy which was delivered in early September. There, His Excellency clearly lays down that there are three ways in which the work of Self-Government in this country must be commenced. The first method is the institution of Local Self-Government. Now when any question of local self-government is discussed, and we are apt to ignore its importance ; it does not catch our imagination; we do not attach that interest to it which the question deserves. And whatever the kind of self-government you succeed in obtaining—and I am sure we will obtain some substantial measure of self-government—be sure that our national work for the next 20 years to come will be in the field of local self-government more than any other. The second road, His Excellency said, must be the filling up of the public offices in this country with more Indians and the third road was by the introduction of some kind of responsible Legislative Councils—and gentlemen, to allay your suspicions —I must confess, we are somewhat suspicious at times—His Excellency said clearly that all this work is to be carried on simultaneously. So, gentlemen, according to His Excellency, you will not be relegated merely to Local Self-Government for many years to come but along with the development of local self-Government you may expect, according to the message of His Excellency, a Legislative Council which is at once representative and responsible.

"RESPONSIBILITY IN POLITICS"

Do not forget, gentlemen, that the word, "responsibility" has got a technical meaning in politics. It does not imply merely moral responsibility. It means that the Government must be responsible to the people of the country, to the electors, *i.e.*, the Legislative Councils will be elected by the people of the country—whatever the extent of the franchise may be, that is a matter of detail which has got to be discussed and no doubt considered carefully. But whatever be the electorate, it is that electorate which will elect members of the Legislative Councils and the Executive Councils will be either elected or taken from the Legislative Councils and the Executive Councils will be responsible not to any outside authority but to the Legislative Councils from which they will be taken and thus ultimately to the people. These are the indications that I find in the statement of the Secretary of State as also in the message of the Viceroy.

SELF-GOVERNMENT FROM MANY VIEW-POINTS

I say, therefore, that the people of this country has got the right now, to expect some kind of responsible self-government in this country and the time has come when we must shake off our apathy and devote our entire energies to the consideration of the question as to the precise form of self-government that we want in this country. The question is a very difficult one and has got to be discussed from a great many points. We have got to consider it from the point of view of our nationality, I mean provincial nationality. We have got to consider this question from a wider outlook. We cannot forget that we live and have been living for many years in the midst of an empire. We cannot forget that the different provinces in India are gradually coming closer to one another and a new nationality which expresses not only the different provinces but the whole of India is growing up in our midst and we cannot forget that our interests, even our selfish interests, our hopes, our ambitions are indissolubly connected with the interest of the empire. These are all the considerations before us. When we sit down to frame a scheme we cannot lose sight of any one of these points.

PROVINCIAL AUTONOMY

If you consider what is the kind of self-government which is exactly necessary for us, what is the first point which suggests itself to you? I will tell you what suggests itself to me. The first thing is provincial autonomy. I desire to explain that expression clearly as far as I understand it, because that expression has been used by many Government officials and by great thinkers in Europe. But

I desire you to approach this question not at all from the European point of view, so far as conception is concerned, but from our own national standpoint. What is the exact meaning of provincial autonomy? I say that the meaning of that expression is that people who have for, hundreds and hundreds of years been living in Bengal have come under the sway of a particular culture, have been animated by a particular genius and the provincial government which will be established in Bengal must give the fullest expression to that ideal. I mean that the Hindus have, for several centuries been living in Bengal and amongst them there have grown up a very great culture which has made itself felt in the domain of science, philosophy, religion, literature and art. It has got a cast of its own; it has got a spirit of its own; it has got a distinct individuality.

When I am speaking of the Hindus of Bengal, I am at once reminded of the Mahomedans of Bengal. They have also lived in Bengal; they have lived with us, by our side and have been surrounded by the same environments and whatever our religious differences may be, there can hardly be any question that their interests and our interests, in point of education, in point of culture, and in point of nationality are the same. When I am speaking of provincial autonomy, I am not forgetting any community or the members of any particular religion. I want to include the whole of them and I say, taking the whole of them, there is a distinct individuality of Bengal. It is on that individual nature that we must take our stand.

Now, gentlemen, provincial government must be so formed that it will not lose the particular interest which that individuality requires. The people of Bengal must realise that the whole of their political enfranchisement must be based upon their ancient ideals and traditions, enlarged no doubt, developed no doubt, modernised no doubt, but still based on those ancient ideals.

BORROWING IDEALS FROM EUROPE

I am not one of those who will borrow all our ideals from Europe. All my life, I have protested against it, I protest against it again and I shall protest against it so long as I live. I am not unmindful of the great culture of Europe. I am not slow in recognising my indebtedness to it but I cannot forget my own individuality. I cannot forget the spirit of Bengal which pervades every thought that I entertain, every hope that I cherish, every fear that I have, and so long as I live, I promise before you to-day that I will devote my life to work out the salvation of the ideal of Bengal. The soul of Bengal had been sleeping for years but directly Self-government is given to us, that soul, while living in an atmosphere of freedom, will make its enormous claim to give the fullest expression to its ideal. I feel sure that the Government cannot but grant us that opportunity—as I hope, the Government will. Gentlemen, I believe that Bengal has a message to give. I feel sure that the day is not distant when the message of Bengal will be delivered and the world will listen.

THE IDEAL TO BE WORKED OUT

Now, gentlemen, this is the ideal of provincial autonomy and how has this ideal to be worked out in practice? We must not rest content with expressing our ideal. We must at once sit down to work to execute that ideal. How do you propose to do it? Different schemes have been put forward. There is the scheme of the 19 members, there is the scheme of the Congress and the Moslem League. There is the scheme of the late Mr. Gokhale. I do not desire to criticise those schemes because it is the universal desire of all our leaders that every district ought to form its own committee to frame its scheme and there should be a conference in Calcutta, where the representatives from all these districts will meet to discuss and deliberate on those schemes, and finally the scheme which is to be presented to the Congress and the League and to the Secretary of State, should be adopted.

PAROCHIAL POLITICS

I do not propose to discuss that in detail at all, but I desire to impress upon you that whatever the scheme you may be pleased to frame, you must not lose sight of what is called parochial politics. From time immemorial the village has been the unit of our national life. You must consider the reconstruction of our village life, you must consider the education of our villagers. You must consider the question as to how they may be represented in the district association, which will be formed with representatives sent by them and you must so frame your scheme—I am merely telling you as to what my individual opinion is—you must so frame it that the interest of what is called parochial government may not in any way suffer from what may be called the interest of the provincial government. Let the village be so connected with the province that it may not be felt as an obstruction but as a real and integral part of the province. Then in considering the representation to the Legislative Council, you will try to so frame your scheme that the interest of the poorest villager as well as that of the richest zemindar may be equally represented; and the interest of the minority may not be neglected.

THE CHARGE OF ILLITERACY

Gentlemen, it has been said, and often said by Anglo-Indians that the great majority of our people are so ignorant, are so illiterate that they cannot be trusted with votes. I do not know, gentlemen, what conclusion you will arrive at, but so far as my own view is concerned, I do not at all agree with that. I do not think that illiteracy and want of education are exactly the same thing. As I know my villagers, I know this that they may be trusted, with the duty of electing persons to represent them in the Legislative Councils. You are more in touch with the villagers than I am—I have seen some of it, but I feel sure that you have got a far more intimate knowledge. I ask you to say whether this is correct that our villager is so ignorant, though he may not be able to read or write, that he does dot know between a bad man and a good man, between a man who will be able to represent his interests properly and a man who will not. I do not think so. And in any scheme which you may draw up, you must make that perfectly clear. I am speaking to this because there is a danger. I do not desire that the mistakes of English history should be repeated in this country. There is no necessity for it. There is no necessity for starting with a very limited franchise and then extending it or having to extend it by civil war afterwards. The history of the Reform Bill in England ought not to be repeated in this country. So, your scheme should be so framed that it must carry within itself the possibility of improvement.

A CENTRAL GOVERNMENT

That is, roughly speaking, my idea of the provincial government. I said that the first thing which should strike us is provincial autonomy. But do not forget that there is a wider interest to consider. These provincial governments must be bound together by a Central Government. I believe it was John Bright who said that the future of India was the United States of India. So far as idea is concerned, it is a grand idea and the idea of provincial autonomy to which I have referred is part of that ideal. But John Bright went further; he said that the several provincial governments should be connected with the British Parliament. To that view I do not assent because the result of that would be that the wider interest of Indian nationality would be overlooked. So we want a central government. What the character of that government is to be, must also be considered *i.e.* how they could have most fully represented all the provincial governments.

AN IMPERIAL FEDERATED GOVERNMENT

Gentlemen, the third need which you must not forget is the need of another Imperial Federated Government to which all the governments of the empire should belong—a Government to which the English Government should belong as one unit, the Indian Government should belong as another, the Government of Africa, Australia and Canada should belong as other units. It will be a sort of federated Parliament. I ask you to consider the grand ideal which is contained in that proposal. I do think in the history of the world there ever was another instance of an empire so vast of an empire, in which so many different races and nationalities and creeds were represented. When you consider all this, you will find what a grand opportunity there is within the British Empire of fulfilling that yet still grander ideal of the federation of the human race. If the federation of the human race is not always to remain the poet's dream, if it is ever to be fulfilled, I feel sure that fulfilment will come through the federation of this vast empire, to which we have the honour to belong.

A WORD OF ADVICE

Well, gentlemen, that is the ideal I put before you and I ask you to consider all this in the scheme which you will frame. But there is one thing to which I desire to draw your attention and it is this; that in framing this scheme you must not be swayed by a feeling that the Government will not grant this, the Government will not grant that. What the Government will grant and what the Government will not grant, that is the business of the Government we have got only to consider what is necessary for our national well-being. We have no doubt got to consider the question of our capacity, but we have got to consider what is necessary for our national well being and if you find that certain steps are absolutely necessary for our national development, do not fail, gentlemen, to put that down in your scheme out of timidity. I ask you not to be timid. Do not be foolhardy, but there is no necessity of being afraid of putting forward the whole of your scheme before the Government. People who are afraid to ask do not deserve. Why should we be afraid to tell the Government that a certain scheme of self-government is necessary for our well-being. The Government invites your opinion. The British Government has declared its policy; the Viceroy has asked you to consider the scheme and do not, for God's sake, spoil that by timidity. Say, there are five items, all of which we want; but let us not ask 2 or 3 of these because the Government will not grant all. I say it is no business of ours and I do not think that at the present moment when the Government is full of that truly imperial idea, when the King's ministers have declared the policy of the Government to grant to this country some kind of responsible self-government, I do not think any scheme which is reasonable, any scheme which is necessary will be refused.

What, if it is refused? Have we not to carry on this fight from year to year, supposing the whole of it is not granted to-day. Have we not to place that scheme before the public—have we not to fight for it year to year, giving the whole of our attention, devoting the whole of our energy to that, and go on fighting till victory is ours? I have seen a great many schemes fail because of our timidity. I ask you to be on your guard because the present is the most opportune moment, because the Government has invited your opinion and in giving your opinion do not think that we ought not to put this or that down because the Government will not accept this.

FOR THE WHOLE OF THE IDEAL

Let us fight for the whole of our ideal. Let us start with this that every cultivator here in this country has got the capacity to judge as to who his representative is going to be. Let us start with this that we can if we only try, if we will only shake off our apathy, do the work of local self-government without the intervention of Government officials. Let us think of this that we are in a position to so form our Legislative Councils, by sending Proper representatives there, that they will carry out our mandate, that they will carry out our ideal and they would elect such an executive that they will do the work which the country requires. Indicate in our scheme how the Provincial Governments will have to be connected with a Central Government. But so far as provincial autonomy is concerned, so far as the different departments of the Executive Government in Bengal are concerned, I should not hesitate to ask for the whole of those powers being transferred to the people of Bengal. Naturally, the Indian Government will retain some powers and I admit it is right that they should retain some powers now at this stage for the task of uniting the different provinces in imperial matters for the purpose of directing the foreign policy and military affairs of the country. But I insist upon you, I implore you, that whatever scheme you may frame, you will not lose sight of the idea that we are capable of governing Bengal, we are capable of carrying on the work which the Executive Council in Bengal does.

THE SYSTEM TO BLAME

Gentlemen, our requirements will not be met by the introduction of a few more of our countrymen into the Civil Service. My quarrel as I said elsewhere, is not with individuals. There are Civil Servants who are honourable men, good men, true men; there may be again those who are not so good—but that would happen in every community. My quarrel is not with the individual at all. My quarrel is with the system. It is the system which is responsible for the bad government of this country. Why is the system bad? It is for this—that there is no responsibility. An English friend of mine has pointed out that. What are the Civil Servants to do? They are not responsible to the people. They have to take their orders from the Executive Council of Bengal. To whom are the members of the Executive Council responsible? Not to the people. They have got to take their orders from the Government of India. To whom is the Government of India responsible? Not to the people. They have got to take their orders from the British Parliament. Has the British Parliament got any time to devote to India? Or to make that responsibility real? No. My Eenglish friend says: they have not. They have neglected India not out of apathy but because their own interest required it—they are to discuss so many questions which are of far greater importance to England than the question of India. So you get a state of things in this country, where the Civil Service, the Executive Council, the Government of Bengal and the Government of India are not responsible to anybody. And under such circumstances, good government is impossible. That is why the Bureaucracy has failed and that is why the Bureaucracy has got to be removed by the introduction of some sort of responsible government—that is why the British Cabinet has suggested the introduction of responsible government. There is no further any question of the failure of the Bureaucracy—that is accepted as a fact, accepted as a fact by people who have the right to know, by people—not ourselves—but people who have the capacity to judge, by people who have political insight and wisdom to come to a correct conclusion. We ought not to waste our energy any more in discussing the question whether this Bureaucracy has succeeded or whether it has failed. It is an accepted fact that it has failed.

The question now is what is the Government that we ought to have. What is the exact character of the representation which we ought to obtain and, gentlemen, I also ask you to consider another thing carefully. In framing the scheme, do not be carried away by mere clamour. It does not matter at all whether your Legislative consists of 100 members or whether it consists of 300 members. It does not matter at all whether the Executive Council will contain two more Indians. What is necessasy to consider is how to make the Legislative Council responsible to the people, how to make the Executive Council responsible to the Legislative Council and how to make this responsible government express the true ideal of the people of Bengal.

HOME RULE MEETING AT BARISAL

A largely attended meeting, presided over by Babu Nibaran Chandra Das Gupta, was held at the Raja Bahadur's Haveli, Barisal, on 14th October 1917, when Mr. C. R. Das spoke as follows :—

Mr. Chairman and gentlemen,—I thank you very much for the kind words that have been said of me this afternoon. I wish I could say that I fully deserve all the kind things which have been said about me by your worthy Chairman. But I will not waste your time by expressing my modesty. I accept this welcome in all humility. I feel in a way to-night which I never felt before.

THE MEMORY OF BARISAL CONFERENCE RECALLED

When I stand here before you, I feel I am standing on a sacred soil. To every Nationalist of Bengal, Barisal is a place of pilgrimage. Here it was that our friend and guru Babu Aswini Kumar Dutt (cheers) has passed the best years of his life in the service of the people of this country and in awakening within them the spirit of nationality in the true light of spirituality. Here it was, gentlemen, that we met at one of the most memorable conferences that took place in Bengal, I mean the Provincial Conference in which we came into conflict with the Executive. I cannot efface from my mind the memory of that meeting. The song of Bande Mataram had been sung before in Bengal but never in that significant way as it was done on that memorable occasion. I remember the conference vividly, the march from this very place to the hall of the conference, the illegal orders that were passed, the illegal arrests that were made, and the voice of the people triumphing over all those illegal attempts on the part of the Executive. Gentlemen, that surely was a landmark in the history of Nationalism and if I have come before you to night to speak of the most momentous question which is agitating the whole country, it is only meet that you should remember the struggles, the glorious fight, the unselfish work and activities of our leaders which have brought us to this state.

SELF-GOVERNMENT AND HOME RULE MEAN THE SAME THING

Now, gentlemen, the question of all questions which we desire to discuss and consider is the question of Self-Government or Home Rule or Swaraj. Both these are mere names. Bombay may call it Swaraj; Madras may call it Home Rule and again Bengal may call it Self-Government—but all these expressions mean the same thing, the same ideal. Once we understand the ideal clearly there will be no further differences as to what it means and what it implies.

HISTORY OF THE GROWTH OF NATIONAL CONSCIOUSNESS IN BENGAL

But before we try to understand the ideal of Self-Government it is as well to take a bird's eye view of the modern history of Bengal which bears upon that momentous question. I shall not weary you by a detailed analysis of that history. But I shall place before you as briefly as I can the landmarks, as it were of that history within which Nationalism was in the making, within which our self-consciousness was growing and which has led us to the present day when the whole country is demanding in one voice, as it were, some sort of responsible self-government. If you do not understand the trend of events and incidents which have led up to this consciousness of nationalism, I am afraid you will miss much that is important to know. Gentlemen, when we talk of the modern history of Bengal, we have to begin with Rajah Ram Mohan Roy (cheers). He was from that point of view, the founder of modern Bengal although I admit that the life work of this great man has got to be re-estimated, revalued, re-understood and reinterpreted. There is no doubt that he was the first who held before us the ideal of freedom. He was the first to sound the note of freedom in every department of life and in all different cultures that have met to-day in India. It may be, we have to modify that, it may be we have to analyse that more carefully and more in details for the purpose of scientific study but it is enough for our purpose to say that he inaugurated many reforms—you might call that reforming activity. He inaugurated the reforms which again, in turn, gave rise to reaction which, again, gave rise to further reforms which made the nation turn on itself till at last, it began to be self-conscious. I do not admit that in the days of the Rajah the nation was self-conscious, but he put before us just the sort of thing which would have helped the immediate awakening of the national consciousness. We cannot but pay homage to that great genius, who, first of all, sounded the note of freedom in politics as well as in other spheres of life. After the death of Rajah Ram Mohan Roy, the work of reform was naturally taken up by the Brahmo Samaj and although a section of our educated people followed the movement, it was principally led by the Brahmo Samaj. That movement was nothing but sounding the same note of freedom, though the ideal of freedom and culture was borrowed from European culture and civilization. With Ram Mohan Roy it was the extension and the Europeanisation of our cultural systems. The same ideal was applied by the Brahmo Samaj to different parts, different provinces of our society.

BANKIM DISCOVERS THE SOUL OF BENGAL

Side by side and almost in parallel lines with that, was another activity which is to be found in the literature of Bengal and principally I refer to the writings of Bankim. You will find that whereas our activity in the domain of reforms followed the European ideals and was a great deal more and more European in its tendencies, the writings of Bankim Chandra Chatterjee shows a different tendency altogether: (A voice: of Bhudeb ?)—and, as I am reminded, also in the writings of Bhudeb —in their writings an attempt was made, though it was not perfect by any means, still an attempt, an honest and sincere attempt was made to discover the soul of Bengal. In that period of our literary history you will find the glorification of Bengal. Bengal was held up as mother and with him. Durga was nothing but the personification, as it were, of Bengal; and in other writings of his you will find an attempt is made to depict though in a somewhat superficial way our national life, to dive deep into the history of our people, into the instincts and culture of our people and find out that which is truly Bengalee and not that which is imported from Europe. All this was in the literature, brewing as it were, and growing in the literature of Bengal but the activities, political and social, were of a different character. I do not know whether it is the result of that literature but gradually it gave rise to an agitation which it is difficult to describe —I mean the reactionary agitation of Sashadhar and his friends. That was a blind movement, an irrational movement it may be, but none the less it was a landmark in the history of the progress of Nationalism. There also you will find the nation began to turn on itself, the nation began to criticise the wealth of culture which was brought from Europe.—Look at it carefully, keenly and try to judge its real value to the people of this country. It was not a rational movement—it started with a hatred of things European, irrational hatred of everything European—but none the less it was a genuine and sincere movement. I desire to be very brief because I am afraid I am tiring you out (Cries of No. No.)

THE MESSAGE OF THE GREAT SWAMI

That movement again in its turn gave rise to the movement of the late Swami Vivekananda. All that was narrow in the movement of Shashadhar was widened, a more liberal note was sounded. The national spirit of which the first note was heard in the movement of Sashadhar, was developed by Swami Vivekananda and in his hands it became a trumpet, I am not saying that the message of the Swami was the final word in our nationalism. It was somewhat abstract in so far as it was more Indian than Bengalee. But it was tremendous—something with an undying glory all its own. If you read his books, if you read his lectures, you are struck at once with his patriotism, love of country, not that abstract patriotism which came to us from Europe but of a different nature altogether a more living thing, something which we feel within ourselves when we read his writings.

THE SWADESHI MOVEMENT

I now pass on to another phase of this national history, that is, the great Swadeshi movement. It really began in 1902. It was intensified in 1905; it went on and I believe, it is still going on. That movement was inaugurated by the same spirit of nationalism made broader, perhaps a little selfish—all national claims begin in national selfishness but made more real. Bengal, for the first time, in those days, realised the [illegible] soul within her. At that time we became fully conscious so far as Bengal is concerned. We turned to the country, the whole of Bengal became to us the symbol of the soul of Bengal. Many of you, gentlemen, must have lived through that period, must have taken part in the many activities of that period and I ask you to say if you ever felt the pulse of the people of Bengal beat so clearly as you did in those days. (Hear, hear) I say before that movement all other movements were more or less borrowed because before that the soul of Bengal was hidden from us. For the first time in the history of our national life that soul began to reveal herself and we were struck with the glory and majesty of it. This period of our national life is remarkable for the writings of Rabindra Nath Tagore (Cheers) and of Bepin Chandra Pal, of D. L. Roy (Cheers) and many others. But at that time our idea of nationalism was centred in Bengal. We never looked beyond Bengal, we were looking at Bengal, we were drinking of Bengal, as it were; and of course, we were enraptured, as all lovers are.

Now, gentlemen, the nationalism of to-day is wider than that. We have lived to grow and we discover that although the soul of Bengal must direct all our activities that although the soul of Bengal must find its fullest expression in every work in which we engage yet there is a wider outlook which cannot be neglected.

THE AWAKENING OF THE CONSCIOUSNESS OF MAHOMEDANS

Before I come to deal with that I should draw your attention to another significant fact and that is, the gradual awakening of the consciousness of the Mahomedan community of Bengal (cheers). At the time of the Swadeshi agitation we were held apart. The self-consciousness which grew within us—the soul of Bengal which revealed herself to us, did not reveal herself to the Mahomedans and we found that they were banded together against this national activity; but, gentlemen, do not be disappointed. You have to view the awakening of the political consciousness of the Mahomedans in Bengal in its true historical perspective, otherwise you will lose sight of much that is important. If you will allow me, I will tell you very briefly something about that history. The literature which would show the wonderful activities of the Mahomedans of Bengal has not yet been unearthed but I have not the least doubt that one day you will find that literature in which both Hindus and Mahomedans joined. Hindus writing in Urdu and Bengalee Mahomedans writing in Sanskrit—I have seen one or two such manuscripts and I am sure there are many such—and when all that literature is unearthed, you will find a wonderful history of Bengalee civilization. In the days of Ram Mohan Roy when English education was introduced in this country, the Mahomedans did not accept it. I am not sorry for that. The Mahomedans did not accept it and they were waiting for a ruder shock. They had forgotten what their forefathers had done in the way of national development. They did not accept English education and at the same time they were divorced from the culture which their fathers had advanced. The result was that whereas the Hindus got on in life, got into government employment, got many things which people value in life, the Mahomedans were left without it and gradually there came to be a sort of estrangement between the two nationalities at the time of the Swadeshi movement. They kept away from that movement and even fought with their might and main against it. Now, gentlemen, I told you I am not sorry for that. I do not remember how I felt it then but now I see that the very attitude which the Mahomedans had taken, that very opposition was the result of their national awakening. We used to deprecate the work of the late Nabob Salimulla in those days because he had organised the Mahomedan opposition to the Swadeshi movement in Bengal. I do not do that now because whatever the form of that activity might have been, Nabob Salimulla succeeded in organising the Mahomedans (cheers). The spirit of nationality spoke amongst the Mahomedans at that time. Once the name is roused I do not care how it is roused. Let it be roused once and then all its narrowness will pass away. All that is true forms part of the national consciousness. What is the result to-day? I went to Dacca and the Mahomedans invited me to an informal conference. When I went there what did I find? Not that estrangement but an intense anxiety on their part to side with the Hindus to combine with the Hindus, (cheers) to fight shoulder to shoulder with the Hindus for working out the real salvation of Bengal (Loud applause). If the Swadeshi Movement was the first step in our national self-consciousness so far as Hindus are concerned, I say it was equally the first step of Mahomedan self-consciousness. Its appearance was against the nation, but its reality was in our favour.

THE MESSAGE OF NATIONALITY

Gentlemen, the message of nationality, as I said before has a wider outlook to-day. We cannot forget that we are living within an empire, perhaps the vastest, the largest and the most glorious empire in the history of mankind. We cannot forget that however truly national we may be—and we ought to be national—under no circumstances should we be divested of our own individuality and I say the Hindus and Mahomedans of Bengal, living together side by side for so many generations, imbibing each other's culture, surrounded by the same atmosphere, the same climate, influenced by the same culture, the two together form the real Bengalee nation. Although we should not lose our own individuality, the spirit of isolation is not the best thing in national life and philosophy.

WE MUST REACH OUT TO THE WORLD

We ought to stand on our own individuality in all the glory which that individuality implies but at the same time we must emerge from that and with the fullest consciousness of ourselves we should reach out to the world. That is the true philosophy of our nationality, and if we are living in an empire to-day, we ought to see that we do not live self-centred, in the splendid isolation of our own individuality. We ought to give the fullest expression to our individuality but we ought to do something more than that. We ought to reach out to the world and how do we reach out to the world? It is by taking our legitimate part in the empire. We should hold fast to this that our individuality should be kept absolutely distinct. I should not give that up for the whole world for if we give that up, we cease to be ourselves. (hear, hear.) But stand on that as we must, we must stretch out our hands across to the world. That we can only do by taking our legitimate part in the activities of this great empire.

PROVINCIAL AUTONOMY—THE FIRST STEP

Gentlemen, the first step in the region of ideal is perfect provincial autonomy. Let us take Bengal. Any form of self-government that we can demand from this point of view must be a government which will secure the autonomy of the Bengalee nation. Then you must not forget that apart from the individuality of Bengal, India as a whole has got a special individuality of its own.

INDIAN NATIONALITY—THE SECOND STEP

We cannot forget that the different nationalities of India, although there are differences between them, although they differ from each other in many respects, yet spiritually and historically they are bound up as so many links in the chain of one living national individuality. We ought not to forget that Bengal, Madras, Bombay and the Punjab are all dominated by one great central culture. The epics of Ramayana and Mahabharata are epics of not only the Punjab, of Bombay, of Madras but also of Bengal and the rest of India. The great religious institutions are common—I am speaking of the Hindus only—to all the provinces, Each province has got a speciality of its own, I admit, but over and above that all these different provinces are bound together in one common culture. If we are to hold fast to our provincial individuality, we must also see that the great individuality of India is not lost. At one time the idea was to develop the different provinces, making the provinces autonomous and to connect these different autonomous provinces with the British Parliament. That will not work out our ideal—that ideal will not allow the great Indian nationality to develop and much as I love Bengal and much as I love my own individuality, my own provincial individuality, I should be sorry indeed if any kind of Self-Government is sought to be introduced into this country which will greatly injure that great ideal of Indian Nationality. If the whole of the Hindu races are bound up in that way, you must also realise that the whole of the Mahomedan races all over India is also similarly bound up together and you must not forget that the two great cultures must meet together, and the result will be a great culture which is not purely

Hindu, not purely Mahomedan but something which is made up of the contact of these two great races. And that is the ideal of Indian Nationality which must be preserved and developed to the fullest extent. If you ask me if I get provincial Self-Government in Bengal, why I should trouble myself about this Indian Nationality.

INDIA MOVING TOWARDS UNITY

In answer I say if I have understood tho lesson of Indian history correctly, I consider that from ages past there was a movement of unifying the whole of India and I think through the many vicissitudes of Indian history, in the time of the Hindus, in the time of Mahomedan rule and now English rule, throughout the many vicissitudes that one idea stands out prominently viz., with each success, with every failure, India was growing more and more and becoming herself. I do not believe that in the old times in the ancient history of our country, there ever was one united India—India was never one whole under the Hindus at any time. I hold in great reverence and veneration all the activities of ancient India. India was great, but the great Indian nationality was in the making. We have profited by what was done in the ancient days, we have inherited all their culture but it is for us to widen that culture for the evolulion of the great Indian nation. That day, gentlemen, is fast approaching. I ask you to consider critically the history of India.

WAS INDIA EVER ONE WHOLE

Can you point your finger to any period of Indian history in which there was an united India? I have failed to discover it. Take the Magadh Empire—that great empire which was built up and which perished in course of time. That empire did not bring out Indian unity to the fullest extent. Take the Mahomedan Empire—it did not—it strove for that and I fully appreciate that, that is the tendency of the Indian history from the earliest time to the present day. (A voice : in the time of Asoke ?) Even in the time of Asoke there was not one whole united India ; it was the domination of one country over the rest of India. The great Indian notionality of which I am speaking was not born then. I am not for belittling the glory of the culture of India under those empires—I have the deepest veneration for them and I say the purpose of Indian history is that throughout the ages, through every success, through every failure, through every battle which was won, through every battle which was lost, the history of India was working out her destiny and turning out the great Indian nation. To-day we see the vision of that glory (cheers). That which could not come to pass under the Hindu kings, that which was not brought about under the Mahomedan gentlemen, it is for us to consider now were we who represent modern India, whether it will be our glorious task to accomplish that if we fail—what of that ?—others will come after us who will achieve this. But achieved it must be (Hear, Hear). The message of India must be given to the world.

The history of India is working out—is bringing out gradually the soul of India and the time will come—we may not live then, our children may not live then,—but I say the day will come when India will stand before the whole world in all her glory of spirituality. The unity of the Hindus and the Mahomedans and of all sects and creeds will be bound together in one great cultural ideal and will influence the civilization of the world (Prolonged cheers). Well, gentlemen, as I am dealing with Self-Government, the point of practical importance which arises is this; that is a scheme of self-government not only should there be perfectly autonomous provincial government but along that such a scheme should be made that all these provincial governments may be united in one central Indian Government because in this our desire for provincial autonomy, we are apt to forget the spirit of the history of India. That is the spirit of nationalism to-day.

FEDERAL GOVERNMENT OF THE EMPIRE THE THIRD STEP

But what of the nationalism of to-morrow?—You have to think of the whole human race, and gradually, some sort of a federal government must be established. It may not be in a few years. It may be a long time yet but some sort of Government must be established, which may be called the Federal government of the whole empire, a government to which the British Parliament will send their representatives, a government to which the Indian Government, after it is federated and after it is nationalised and after it is made responsibe, will also send her representatives,—a government to which Australia will send her representatives—a government to which Africa will also send her representatives.

FEDERATION OF ALL NATIONS THE GOAL

That is the future federal government of the British Empire and I say that as an ideal, we should cling to that and cling to that because we must not forget that the ultimate goal of human activity in every country is what the poet has described, a Parliament of nations, the federation of the world. That is an ideal which has got to be worked out. The time is coming when a definite scheme should be framed to work out as far as possible this great ideal.

THE DECLARATION OF THE SECRETARY OF STATE.

Gentlemen, many of you may have read the declaration of Policy issued by the Secretary of State the other day and may also have read the speech of His Excellency the Viceroy made with reference to that. Reading these two statements together, it is clear that the time has come when every educated man in this country should set about earnestly to frame a scheme for the introduction of self-government keeping in mind the ideal which we have before us and keeping in mind also the standard of practical politics. Now, gentlemen, if you have to frame a scheme like that, you will of course take into consideration the first point, *viz.*, of provincial autonomy *i.e.*, of each province. Let us think of Bengal at the present moment, Bengal must have a government which is representative that is to say, the people of Bengal will be the electors and they will elect their representative to this Government and the legislative Council is to regulate and control the executive. The Government officials that there are at the present moment, will be under the control of that Executive Department or in other words, every office and the government itself will be responsible to the people of this country. That is the first point you will have to consider. You will have to consider how you can bring about these things, the particular method according to which this must be worked out. Now, gentlemen, the second thing that you have to consider is how to federate these different provinces and connect them with the Central Government. These are the two important points which you have got to think about at the present moment and I invite your attention to a scheme which you must formulate amongst yourself. I have given you what my views are but you are not bound by these; you must form a committee of competent men to frame such a scheme and I think all the representatives of the districts should meet in Calcutta some time in November to discuss the scheme of self-government. We shall then adopt one scheme for Bengal in which the interests of the Hindus and the interests of Mahomedans will all be considered and we, the Hindus and Mahomedans of Bengal will present this scheme to the Secretary of State when he arrives here in November or in December.

DIFFICULTIES AHEAD

Gentlemen, I have told you what the ideal is according to my view, and I ask you to set about working it out. But you must not be negligent of the difficulties that lie in your way. And the first and foremost of these difficulties is the agitation of the Anglo-Indians who have formed themselves into the European Association for the purpose of trying their best to defeat the noble object of the Government of India (Shame, shame). Gentlemen, so far as the Government is concerned, it has declared its policy openly and clearly and if the European Association sets itself against this noble desire of the Government of this country it would be our clear duty to stand against the mischievous activity of the Association. (Hear, hear.) Gentlemen, I have dealt with their speeches and the absurdly exaggerated claims which they have made, at other places. I do not desire to repeat them again but you will find that these speeches are all couched in violent laguage and sobriety and judgment is conspicuous by its absence in almost all the utterances made at that meeting in Calcutta.

RACIAL RANCOUR

They have started this agitation by vilifying our leaders and attacking both the ideal and the method of the Home Rule movement of this country and I charge that the result of that is racial rancour which I say, it ought to be the endeavour of every honest citizen, be he Indian or be he European, or be he Anglo-Indian, to avoid. Gentlemen, I desire to give you just one or two specimens of that. This is how Sir Archy Birkmyre speaks of the activities of the people I quote from his speech:—

> "We should have been content to treat this agitation (i.e., our agitation) with the contempt it deserves, but we are confronted with the alarming fact that the Government is hauling down its colours before these lawless agitators."

Gentlemen, this statement professes contempt not only for the activities of the people, the unselfish and honest activities of the leaders of the people of this country but it also professes contempt for their own Government, (Cries of shame) as it refers to the actions of the Government, the noble actions of the Government in these words;

"But we are confronted with the alarming fact

that the Government is hauling down its colours before these lawless agitators"

ARE WE LAWLESS AGITATORS?

Gentlemen, our agitation is described as the agitation of lawless people I read through these speeches very carefully and I challenge any one of the speakers to find out a single utterance in Mrs. Beasant's speeches on the question of Home Rule, in her many pamphlets on this subject which may be characterised as violent. I challenge them to find out a single sentiment in any one of these utterances of Mrs. Besant which stands for lawlessness. I have read them carefully; these Anglo-Indian agitators have not. I have read them carefully and I say that Mrs. Besant has laid down clearly and emphatically that the agitation for Home Rule must be carried on lawfully and by the use of argument not by the use of methods which are against law. She has laid that down so often in her speeches that anybody who refers to that agitation as lawless has no excuse for such ignorance.

WHO ARE VIOLENT—WE OR YOU?

I will now give you another bit from the same speaker:—

"Most of you are aware of the quality or the language used by the Indian agitator when he wishes to libel British rule."

The quality of language used by the Indian

agitator indeed! Well, gentlemen, you have read the speeches of these Anglo-Indian agitators and you have read the speeches of Indians who have addressed the country from time to time on the question of Home Rule. I ask you to compare the tone of these speeches and I ask you to say who are violent—they or we? I will give you one choice bit from Mr. Wigett. He says:—

"Can any one here say that in releasing Mrs. Besant the Government of India has exercised that power in a matter that we have a right to expect. . . . . It is a direct invitation to further noisy and blatant upheavals of violent passion."

Well, that is the language of moderation. I shall pass by that without a comment.

"SPLENETIC BITTERNESS OF A POLITICAL SECT"

I will give you another from this gentleman's speech. Referring to the writings of Indians on the question of Home Rule and in support of our claim for Home Rule, this gentleman says:—

"Such writings do not represent the feelings of the people of Calcutta, or anything indeed but the splenetic bitterness of a political sect."

That is very choice language, gentlemen, "splenetic bitterness of a political sect." That is very moderate language indeed! I shall pass by this also without any comment. I come now to Mr. F. W. Carter.

OUR "UNSCRUPULOUS" METHODS

Referring to our activity, he says:—

"Unscrupulous methods and audacious claims of a few noisy agitators."

Mark the words—"unscupulous methods and audacious claims." Our claims are audacious because we want to govern ourselves because we say that for the last 150 years there has been a bureaucratic form of government—bureaucracy has been tried and found wanting. This is an admitted fact now, admitted by politicians in England and by politicians in India—admitted by implication in the statement of the Secretary of State and the speech of His Excellecy the Viceroy. That the Bureaucracy will no longer do and because we saw that the bureauoracy must be replaced by some sort of government which is self-government and which is responsible to the people of this country. We are told of the unscrupulous methods and the audacious claims of a few noisy agitators. That again is language of moderation and calculated to create (A voice: and preserve)—yes and preserve a "calm atmosphere." The idea of these Anglo-Indian agitators is this: that when they speak of us they can use the most violent language, they can incite racial bitterness they can say whatever they like with the most perfect impunity but if any agitators, if any Indian patriot refers in the slightest degree to the evils of bureauratic government in this counrry, they are at once a noisy lot who must be punished by the government.

ADDING INSULT TO INJURY

I give you another passage from Sir Archy Birkmyre again:—

"Of the loyalty and devotion of the fighting races of the Punjab, Sir Michael Odwyer has spoken in terms which everyone of us in this room will cordially endorse. But the spirit of the Punjab has not been manifested in other provinces." Gentlemen, so far as Bengal is concerned—and this speaker was speaking amidst Bengalees, so far as Bengal is concerned, I say, for anybody to charge that Bengal has not contributed to the war by money or by manpower is a libel on the whole Bengalee race. I say it is adding insult to injury. When did you allow the Bengalees to wear arms? When was it for the first time that you called upon them to wear arms and to go and fight our enemy? It was only the other day. Do you expect, does any reasonable man who wants to put forward reasonable argument expect that a whole people who have suddenly been called upon to take arms and march against an enemy, that they will at once, as if by a magic, turn out a very large army? Whose is the fault? Is it the fault of Bengal that today you do not find thousands and thousands, lacs and lacs of Bengalees fighting for the empire? Whose is the fault? You deprive them of their arms, you tell them that they are enemies (shame, shame), you declare to the world that they were never fit for military service and when suddenly you call upon them to take arms and fight, can anybody say that Bengal has not responded to the call sincerely, earnestly and if I may say, valiantly ? I say a speech of this description is adding insult to injury. That is what these speakers say of the people of Bengal. Let me now place before you one or two passages which show their attitude to the government of this country when the government has resolved upon doing justice to the people of this country.

"MEDDLING MUDDLERS"

I quote from the speech of the Hon. Mr. Ironside. It is rather a long quotation but I am afraid that I must place this before you to bring out the quality of Anglo-Indian agitation. I hope you will bear with me. He says :—

"At any rate, we don't want any from the House of Commons, and I would commend this remark to Mr. Montagu, for we distrust them root and branch. At this distance we watch the unhealthy game which proceeds at Westminster and to honest men it is enough to make one weep for one's country; and I think, you will agree with me, gentlemen, that we have none of it here. This is no time for meddling, least of all from a representative of a Ministry who one and all by their words and deeds brought the old country to the verge of internal ruin, vilified honest men and patriots slithered into unprepared, and having made a mess of everything have hung on to their self-elected posts like limpets until a second time the destruction of the empire was nearly effected, We are not taking the same risk here. Mr. Montagu, I believe, started in a department created for the definite purpose of helping to win the war. Had it been of any use, I presume, he would have stayed there but being one of a party of a meddling muddlers, he has found his way back to the Indian Office."

This is language of moderation applied to the Secretary of State for India who is entrusted by the British Parliament with the government of this country. I can assure you gentlemen if anything half as violent as that had been said by any one of us, this gentleman would have been furious and would have exhibited his fury ten times more; and the "Statesman" newspaper would have said that speakers who make use of such language should be punished by the State so that their speeches may not create disaffection. But when you call the Secretary of State a meddling muddler, I suppose that is allowable. When you heap contempt upon the whole of the British Parliament, I suppose it is allowable. If only an Indian says that the bureaucratic Government has been found to be wanting, it has failed in its duties, it has failed in its charge of the administration of this country, it is such violent language that the State must put down.

ANGLO-INDIANS TEACH THE HOUSE OF COMMONS

Then the same speaker goes on to say:

"You must remember that we have to teach the House of Commons before we can gain their ear and support."

I hope the House of Commons will be enlightened by the lessons which it gets from speakers of this description. (Loud laughter).

WHO BRINGS GOVERNMENT TO CONTEMPT

To turn again to Mr. Wigget—he says:—

"What an extraordinary spectacle!" referring to the release of Mrs. Besant and the regret expressed by Sir Michael O'Dwyer,

'Of a sentimental weak-kneed Government'

If this is not showing contempt for the Government I do not know what contempt is. This is not all: there is an alarming fact expressed in some of these speeches. Some of the speakers have stated that the civil servants and the military officers are entirely in sympathy with them in their resistance to any kind of self-government being granted to this country.

ARE THE MEMBERS OF THE CIVIL AND MILITARY SERVICES WITH ANGLO-INDIANS?

Gentlemen, I shall place before you one passage from the speech of Mr. Carter and another from the speech of Sir A. W. Binning.

Mr. Carter says :—

"I appeal, therefore, to the Government on behalf of all Europeans whether engaged in trade and commerce or serving in Government employment .....I assure the Government that they are here in spirit."

Gentlemen, the Civil Servants were present in spirit at this meeting according to the statement of Mr. Carter! (Laughter).

And the other speaker says this :—

"Our claims, as put forward at present, will have the silent, but none the less effective, support of the Indian Civil Service and Military officers whose lot is cast in this country and who equally with us, view with grave apprehension the measures which we fear, on effort will be made to force on us."

Now, gentlemen that is absolutely startling. For myself, I refuse to believe this. I refuse to believe that the members of the civil service and the military officers who are servants of the King should so far forget themselves that they should express their sympathy with these Anglo Indian agitators, express their views to them against the policy which has been declared by His Majesty's Government. I say, I refuse to believe this because if it were true, it discloses an alarming state of things. It shows this: that whatever the policy of the British Government may be, whatever the policy and the declaration of His Majesty's Government may be, His Majesty's servants in India may so combine and may so actively oppose people who stand up for that policy as perhaps to render that policy nugatory. I say, if it is true, it discloses an alarming state of things and I hope the Government will take note of the speeches and make an enquiry into this and if there is any truth in this statement, I ask the Government why should they allow their own servants to so conduct themselves as to represent unnecessary opposition to the declared policy of the Government. (Hear hear).

WHAT IS ANGLO-INDIANS CLAIM

Now, gentlemen, I have referred to the speeches to show to you how unreasonable in spirit, how violent in language those speeches were. But what is their claim? Why is it that just after the declaration of this policy by the Secretary of State in August and the speech of the Viceroy in September that they should assemble in a meeting and oppose that policy tooth and nail. The declaration contained only this: that some sort of responsible government is to be introduced in this country—nothing beyond that. Why is it that all the Anglo-Indians gathered together and began to denounce that policy before the details are published or worked out? What is the claim which they make? I shall read to you from the speech of Sir Archy Birkmyre which puts forward what that claim is. This worthy gentleman says:

"The greater part of the commerce of India the

basis of her prosperity is controlled and financed by Britishers."

Mark the word gentlemen, "Britishers" not the Anglo-Indian community alone but the Britishers. He goes on:

"All the progress that India has made in recent generations is due almost entirely to British direction, British capital and British enterprise. The men who are responsible for the vast interests created by the British in India cannot sit down voiceless and idle when the danger confronts us that these interests will be sacrificed to appease the political appetites of mob orators and Home Rulers."

Does it stand to this that the introduction of any kind of self-government in this country, however safeguarded the different interests may be, means such a disregard of the interests of these Anglo-Indian Agitators that the Government must be forced to give up its honest desire of introducing such a government? I ask in all seriousness does the claim go so far as this?—The Anglo-Indian claim which is put forward at this meeting does it go so far to insist that no kind of self-government, however limited it may be, however safeguarded the different interests in the country may be, that no kind of self-government is to be introduced at all into this country because these Anglo-Indians brought money in the shape of capital to this country—a statement which requires examination—because they brought capital to this country that India must forever be destitute, must forever be deprived of any measure of self-government? If this is their claim, it is so preposterously unreasonable that it requires no refutation at all. But gentlemen, the claim is curiously worded.

DO ANGLO-INDIANS REPRESENT THE BRITISH NATION?

It is not a claim put forward on behalf of Anglo-Indians alone but it is a claim put forward on behalf of the Britishers, it is a claim by the people of England. I deny these Anglo-Indian agitators' right to represent the people of England. I deny that they have got any right to say anything on behalf of the people of England. If any plebiscite is taken to-day in England, I feel sure that there would be a vast majority in favour of the introduction of Self-Government to this country (Hear, hear.)

MUST WE BE DENIED HOME RULE BECAUSE YOU HAVE BROUGHT CAPITAL?

If this claim is based on the mere fact of their introducing capital in this country, you have to consider whether they have not been sufficiently profited by the introduction of such capital. Does it mean this then that because people bring capital to this country, because they find it profitable to do so, they would have the right to say to the Government: you shall not introduce Self-Government in this country? Have they the right to tell the people: look here, we have brought capital to this country, therefore, you shall not have any desire to quarrel with these Anglo-Indian agitators. We do not regard politics from that utterly selfish point of view from which they regard it,

THEIR ONLY CLAIM IS ADEQUATE REPRESENTATION

I am free to admit in any scheme of Self-Government which is framed and which is accepted by the people and the Government of this country, these Anglo-Indian merchants ought to be allowed to be represented, that is to say, I do not desire that any scheme should be framed which would disregard the interests of any class of people, whether Hindu, Mahomedan or Anglo-Indian, whatever the basis of the franchise may be. But I say that these people have got no right to dictate to the Government of India and to the people alike that they shall not have Self-Government. I ask my Anglo-Indian friends to consider this question from a little higher point of view. They must see that India cannot ever remain without Self-Government. They must see that at some time or other the voice of the people is bound to be heard and if they do their duty by this country, by which they have been profited to a very large extent, they ought to help in this work of Self-Government rather than oppose it. I call upon them again to stand on a higher platform and consider the question of Self-Government not in this way but more seriously and with more consideration for the interest of the people of this country.

STIRRING UP CONFLICTING INTERESTS

Now, gentlemen, there is another difficulty to which I must also refer, When there are so many conflicting interests in this country it may be that particular classes of people will be instigated to stand up against Home Rule. I blame no one in particular but I am placing before you a possible difficulty. Interested people may stir up the Namasudras and tell them "Look here, you are hated and oppressed by the people, the Hindus of Bengal, why should you assist them and help them to bring in Self-Government because if Self-Government is granted, the Hindus are bound to oppress you all the more?" Advisers may be found who will go to my Mahomedan brethren and tell them: "you are as yet backward in education, if Self-Government is granted to Hindus why they will be more powerful than you and they will look down upon you and oppress you." Endeavours of that description unfortunately are not uncommon in this country and at such a momentous period of our history the same attempts might be repeated. Gentlemen, it is your duty, under these circumstances, you who are educated to go to your less educated brethren, Hindus or Mohomedans and to expose before them the fallacy of any such argument.

THERE WILL BE NO ROOM FOR OPPRESSION IN OUR SCHEME OF SELF-GOVERNMENT

You ought to tell them that self-government does not mean the Self-Government of the Hindus; Self-Government does not mean the Self-Government of the Mahomedans; Self-Government does not mean the Self-Government of the Zemindars; Self-Government means Government by all the people of Bengal in which all interests are to be represented and if there are any classes who are depressed or oppressed, they ought to be told that the sooner self-government is introduced into this country the better for them (Hear hear): they ought to be told that we haveno desire to restrict the franchise in any manner at all to the disregard of any such interest and if any kind of responsible government is introduced into this country, which is made responsible to the people, they will have the power in their hands to oppose any oppression or injustice in every possible way. They will have the power to return their friends to the Legislative Councils they will have the power to tell the people who oppose them: if you want to oppress us, if you go on in that way, it would be against the work of national development and you shall not have the power to do that. We are asking for putting the power into the hands of the people and are we to be told that these people for whom we are fighting in whose interest we are fighting for the last 30 years, that we are likely to disregard the interest of these people?

THE TEEMING MILLIONS ARE OF US

If we are not fighting for the teeming millions of India, can anybody tell me whom we are fighting for? Am I fighting for myself? If I am selfish, why should I bother about self-government? Why can I not attend to my profession, make money and go home and sleep? Why should I go all over the country and demand Home Rule which is the only means of uplifting the teeming millions of our country if I have not their interest at heart? If anybody says that the Nationalists who are fighting for Home Rule are doing so in their own interest I fling the lie to the slanderers teeth. I say we are engaged in a noble task and we shall not rest content unless such a kind of self-government is granted to this country which will keep alive the interest of every community, which will regard and safeguard the interest of every class of people in Bengal. We belong to the same race. They are of us. God give us strength to fight their battle! (Prolonged Cheers.)

(Amrita Bazar Patrika.)

PROTEST AGAINST INTERNMENTS

Under the Presidency of Mr. Chakravarthy, there was an enthusiastic meeting of the citizens of Calcutta, in the Town Hall, on 5th March, 1918 when Mr. C. R. Das spoke as follows :—

Mr. Chairman, Ladies and Gentlemen, I feel thankful to you for giving me this opportunity to raise my voice in protest against this arbitrary and unjust piece of legislation. Indeed I feel at this moment that no argument is necessary to convince you of the injustice of this measure. Mr. Chakravarty has dealt with it so fully and elaborately and has put before you all the considerations with reference to this matter with such force and lucidity that it seems unnecessary to continue this argument. I will therefore take up the resolution which has been entrusted to me and place it before you with a few observations which I have to make. The resolution consists of 5 clauses. (Mr. Das then read the resolution.)

I will deal with the third clause first, because it admits in my opinion of no discussion at all. Take all the arguments which had been advanced by His Excellency's government; accept them all. And even then there can be no justification for the present policy of the Government. (Hear, hear.) Either there is evidence against these interned persons or there is no evidence. If there is no evidence against them there is an end of the matter at once. And if there is evidence against them, what justification can there be in not bringing them to trial? It only makes people suspicious that there is not sufficient evidence against them. If there is sufficient evidence what justification can there be, I repeat, in not placing them instantly before a court of justice for trial? The argument that the present machinery of justice is insufficient is an argument which no body believes. I say it will be a dangerous thing if the idea goes abroad that people are kept in jail, in police custody without being brought to trial, while the Government has evidence against them. I say it will be a dangerous thing if this idea goes abroad, because people will at once come to the conclusion that probably there is no such evidence which can secure conviction in a court of justice. I cannot conceive of a more dangerous consequence.

Let me now deal with the other clauses of the resolution. I am one of those who never believe in tinkering in the matter of legislation. Either this measure is just or unjust. If it is unjust, there can be no ground for keeping it on the statute book. The Chairman has put this case very clearly before you. He describes this Act as "lawless law." Hear hear). I want you to fully realise the meaning of that observation made by the distinguished chairman. I say that, behind that observation lies the fundamental objection which we have got against the Act. What is "lawless law"? Any law which is not based upon justice, of which the object is not to serve and secure that justice upon which the stability of society depends, must necessarily be "lawless law." It is something which is put forward under cover of law, which is not law, which offends again every principle of justice, which is a negation of justice and therefore negation of law (cheers.) We protest against this Act because it offends the fundamental rights of man. (Hear, hear) To be taken and kept in custody for an indefinite period of time without being told what evidence there is and without being brought to justice according to the law of the land ('shame, shame') is a denial of the primary rights of humanity. (Hear, hear.) This is "lawless law" (prolonged cheers.)

You must realise what this Act is. I desire to read some portions of it to you, because many of you are not lawyers and probably do not know what grim injustice lies behind the apparently innocent expressions which you find in this Act. It is called the Defence of India Act—an Act for the public safety and yet public safety is nowhere defined. It is a vague generality (Hear, hear.) The public denounce it (hear, hear) people do not want it (hear, hear.) Is it to be forced down the throat of the public—this Act which is based upon grievous and intolerable injustice? (Cries of 'no' no'—loud cheers).

Let us follow the text of the law still further. This Act gives power to certain officials "civil or military,"—when in the opinion of such authority there are reasonable grounds for suspecting that any person has acted, is acting or is about to act in a manner prejudicial to the public safety to direct that such persons shall not enter, reside or remain in any area specified in writing by such authority or that such person shall reside and remain in any area so specified or that he shall conduct himself in such manner or abstain from such act, etc., etc. How beautifully vague! (Hear, hear.) These are admittedly innocent words; and when the Act was passed was there any one amongst us present here to-day who had the slightest idea of the use to which this Act might be put? Who at that time ever dreamt that this Act would be used for taking away young lads from their homes, keeping them in prison for days and months, keeping them in solitary cells and for putting them to indignity after indignity? Was this the intention of the legislature when it was passed? One can understand a war measure, one can understand that drastic legislation is necessary at the time of war when the enemy is at the gate. But is it just to take away young lads from their homes, from their mothers' arms, as it were (shame, shame) and keep them imprisoned ('shame,' 'shame') without telling them why, without bringing them to justice ('shame,' 'shame'—loud cheers)? Is any argument necessary to demonstrate that such an act is oppressive and must be abrogated? (Hear, hear —loud cheers). The answer is necessity, which Lord Morley has characterised as the old familiar plea of tyrants, (shame, shame, hear, hear—loud cheers). Law is necessary for the preservation of society (Hear, hear,) but not this thing which you call law (Cheers) Could any law be more arbitrary, more unjust than this Act? (Cries of 'no.') I ask you to consider this plea of necessity again. Surely it is not for defending India against the enemy, not for defending Bengal which has suffered most under this oppressive legislation (Cries of 'shame,' 'no,' 'no'). People who suffer and groan under this repressive legislation may easily misread and misunderstand your real object and think that it was intended to crush that hunger for liberty, which no bureaucratic government can tolerate for one single moment (loud cheers).

This policy as the Chairman has reminded you began in 1905 with those illegal circulars which you may remember. Those circulars then, as you all know, led to a good deal of misunderstanding. There were circulars against the shouting of 'Bandemataram' and various circulars directed against students. Some people thought that the object of these circulars was also to prevent our self development and to suppress our growing hunger for liberty (loud applause). I ask the Government, can you blame the people who suffer from such injustice, if they misunderstand your object and misconstrue your action? (loud cheers.)

We feel it is our bounden duty to raise our voice of protest against this Act. The object ascribed is wrong. What is the real object? They say "there is a vast conspiracy in the country." My answer is I admit it I know and believe and I am sure of it as sure as I am standing here to-night, that there is a revolutionary party in Bengal. But what then ? Do you think that you will be able to suppress that revolutionary party in that way? Has revolution ever been checked by unjust legislation ? Give me one instance from history where the Government has succeeded in putting down revolutionary movements by oppressive legislation. I admit that the thing is an evil. I admit that the activity of the revolutionary party is an evil in this country which has to be eradicatted, But what is the duty of the Government ? Is it not their duty to take such step as will effectually eradicate it ? (Hear, hear.) Does the Government really believe that the revolutionary party wants any other foreign power in this country ? (Cries of 'no' 'no'). I venture to think that they do not. If not, what do they want ? Has the Government ever enquired into the causes which led to that revolutionary movement? From 1905 we have been hearing of it, up to now repressive measure after repressive measure has been passed (cries of shame, shame), but has any attempt of any kind whatsoever been made to discover the real causes of this revolutionary movement? (Cries of 'no' 'no'). I may tell you as I have told many of those in authority that

I know more about these people than probably anybody else in this hall. I have defended so many of the cases, and I know the psychology of their mind, I know the cause of this revolutionary movement is nothing but hunger for freedom. (Hear, hear.) Within the last 150 years what have you done to make the people of this country free or even really fit for freedom? Do we not constantly hear that we are not fit for self-government ('shame' 'shame') that we are illiterate, that we are not sufficiently educated? (shame, shame.) May I retort by asking "you have been here for the last 150 years, with best of motives, with the object of making us fit for self-government? Why is it then that you have done nothing to this end?" (loud cheers).

This is the psychology of the revolutionary movement. Our educated young men see that nations all over the world are free. They compare their position with the position of other nations, and they say to themselves "why should we remain so? We also want liberty." (Cheers). Is there anything wrong in that desire? Is it so difficult to understand their point of view? Do we not all know this hunger for liberty? These young men burning with the enthusiasm of youth feel that they have not been given any opportunity of taking their legitimate part in the government of their country, in shaping the course of their national development. Give them that right to-day, you will hear no more of the revolutionary movement (loud cheers). "Give them that right to-day, tell the people of this country here it is, we mean to change the system of Government, the government will be yours (loud cheers) government of the people and by the people, work for the good of our country, build up your nationality, shape the course of your history" (loud and prolonged cheers), and I guarantee that from the next day the revolutionary party will cease to exist (Hear, hear, loud and prolonged cheers), I have said this. Our leaders have said this over and over again to those in authority, but we have not been listened to.

On the contrary we are told that the only remedy is the Defence of India Act. ('shame,' 'shame'), We have been told that political crimes have decreased, since the passing of this Act. I say it is not so. Overtacts are not the only measure of political crimes. How could political crimes have decreased when disaffection has increased? (Hear, hear). Members of the revolutionary party may remain grim and silent, but I am sure every case of internment under this Act increases the volume of discontent and disaffection in this country. Does not that strengthen their hands? This is the real danger (Hear, hear). It is acting like poison and eating into the vitals of our nationality (Hear, hear). I protest against this Act as it is a menace to our liberty (Hear, hear), I protest against this Act as it is a menace to our loyalty to the empire to which we belong. (Hear, hear, loud and prolonged cheers).

There are people in this country who will tell you that the Government will never repeal this Act, So my countrymen I say, "Do not be disheartened." (Hear, hear). I believe in my heart of hearts that once the people of this country unite and raise their voice, the voice of a united nation, there is no power on the face of the earth which can resist it, (loud and prolonged cheers). Let us all say "Repeal this Act, we will not have it." (Hear, hear). Let this cry reach the country, every village, every town; let this meeting be followed up by hundreds and thousands, let us all be united in our demand for the repeal of this Act and I say this Act shall be repealed, (loud and prolonged cheers).

INDIAN DEPUTATION TO ENGLAND

(Under the Presidency of Babu Motilal Ghose, a public meeting of the Citizens of Calcutta was held on the 18th March, 1918, at Professor Ramamurti's Pavilion, Bow Bazar Street, to support the Indian Deputation to England, when, Mr. C. R. Das in moving the resoluion "That this public meeting accords its hearty support to and records its full approval of the deputation, consisting of among others of Lokamanya Bal Gangadhar Tilak, the Hon'ble Mr. G. S. Khaparade, Babu Bebin Chandra Pal, the Hon'ble Mr. B. V. Narasimha Iyer, Mr. Manjeri Ramier, Mr. Syed Hussain, Mr. G. Joseph, Mrs. Sarojini Naidu, Mr. N. C. Kelkar, Mr. R. P. Karandikar, Babu Jitendralal Banerjee and Pandit Iqbal Narayan Gurtu," spoke as follows):—

Gentlemen,—There are two points which are involved in this resolution. The first is about the fitnesss of the gentlemen whom we have selected. I need hardly say that these gentlemen are in the highest sense the representatives of this country and I have not the least doubt that if the votes of our countrymen were taken—the votes of the uneducated and the educated, of all classes and communities in this country,—there cannot be the least doubt that every one of these gentlemen would have been elected.

Then comes the question why are we sending these gentlemen to England at a time when the journey is not safe. The answer to that question is not very difficult. We are passing through a very critical period in our history. We feel, every one amongst us who thinks of his country feels, that self-government cannot be delayed any longer. If self-government is denied to us it is certain that the growth of our nationality, and the development of Indian manhood will all be stopped. It is a matter of absolute necessity that within a short time, I say within one year or two, we must have self-government (cheers)—government responsible to the people—or we cannot exist as a nation. Now, what are the impediments? We have found out in the course of the last 30 years that the Bureaucracy in this country will not grant us anything which is at all substantial. Gentlemen, on one occasion I had the hardihood to say this before a high official and I was asked why did I say it. I will tell you what my answer was. I said and I repeat that within the last 30 years there never has been a reform proposed which had not been opposed and defeated by the Bureaucracy (hear, hear). If you consider for one moment the history of the last 30 years what do you find? You find that the noble policy of Lord Ripon was opposed by the Bureaucracy, you find that local self-government for which Lord Ripon fought, although nominally granted to us, was in reality denied to us. If you consider again such a simple reform as the separation of the Executive and the Judiciary what do you find? You find that Viceroy after Viceroy recommended it. You find statesman after statesman in England recommended it; yet, what is it which has prevented such a useful reform being put through ? My answer is, it is the Bureaucracy in this country. (Shame, shame). Think again of Lord Morley's reforms which is called the Minto-Moreley reforms. I said to this high official that this scheme was something when it left the shores of England, but it became absolutely ridiculous when it got into the hands of the Indian Bureaucracy (Shame, shame.) I was then asked why did I say so ? My answer was and my answer is because I have not got a vote under that scheme and I pointed out that Sir S. P. Sinha, who was considered worthy enough to be appointed a member of the Executive Council was not a qualified voter either (shame, shame). Under these circumstances are we not justified in saying that that scheme was rendered absolutely ridiculous when it got into the hands of the Indian Bureaucracy ? (cheers.)

It is plain, therefore, that you may agitate as long as you like; youmay demand your right, as you have a right to demand, but you will not get the Bureaucracy in this country to support you. You must, therefore, go to their masters. Our demands must be carried across the seas to the great British

Democracy (cheers). We want to be told why is it that we are not fit for self-government? I have said on other occasions that I do not ask for any particular kind of right which requires any elaborate consideration. I want the right which every nation on the face of the earth has—the right to build up our own constitution (cheers). I do not care about the details of the scheme just now. You can discuss them fully when the time comes. The question at present is a very simple one. I want our representatives to go to England, and tell the British Democracy that, we want nothing more, nothing less, than, the right to build up our own constitution,—a constitution which alone will enable us to secure the development of our nationality, a constitution which is absolutely necessary for the development of our manhood. Our representatives must go to England and tell the British people that the men on the spot are no longer to be trusted (hear, hear)—they must plead our case and they must insist on our rights (cheers).

If we find that we are not to get self-government; we have at least the right to get an honest answer. Let the British Democracy say if it likes, that this war is a war of liberation of humanity, but liberation of humanity does not include the liberation of India. If that is the view of the British Democracy let them tell us so. We won't be content with excuses and pretences. Gentlemen, when I consider the objections put forward to the grant of self-government, I can hardly keep my patience. What is it that they say? They say we are not educated enough to get self-government. My answer is: whose fault is it? For the last 150 years you have been governing this country, and yet you have not succeeded in educating the people of this country to such an extent that they may be fit for governing themselves. Do we not know that Japan was made only in 50 years? You have had 150 years. Why is it that at the end of that period we are told that we are not fit to govern ourselves? The very statement fills us with apprehension. As days go by, we will be rendered more and more unfit. No gentlemen, nobody really believes that the time has not come. It is a matter of immediate necessity and we must have it (cheers).

Then we are told, we are divided between many sects. We follow different religions, we have got different interests to serve and so on. Arguments are piled upon arguments in this way—it is always easy to argue and we at any rate who belong to the profession of law, know that it is always possible to argue. (Laughter). We all know that though vanquished, one can argue still (laughter) But do we not know, from the history of civilization, that directly you make people of different classes, of different religions, and of different interests, work together, work for a common good, do we not find that unity is brought about more successfully from the very fact of having to work together than by any other means? Therefore if you say that we are not fit for Self-Government, because we are divided in our interests, and in our religons my answer is that self-government and self-government alone is the remedy of that. (Hear, hear.)

Then we are told that there is a revolutionary party amongst us and therefore we cannot be trusted with self-government. I have said elsewhere and I say again that I am not one of those who deny that there is a revolutionary party. But if you consider that question for the moment, you find that the only remedy which is possible, the only remedy which will effectually eradicate the revolutionary movement, is, the grant of self-government (loud cheers). I say this to the Government—you have been troubled over this revolutionary movement for so many years now—you suspected it in 1905. Have you ever made any effort to understand the psychology of that movement? Have you ever appointed any commission to enquire into the causes of this revolutionary movement? No. And yet, we have to take it that you want to eradictate it by repressive legislation (shame). My answer is that repressive legislation can never put an end to a revolutionary movement—it is only by satisfying their legitimate desire, it is only by satisfying their hunger, as I said the other day, for liberty that you can put an end to it. If you understand that problem you will find that the sooner self-government is introduced into this country it is better. I say it is better not only from the point of view of us Indians, it is better from the point of view of the British Democracy also, and that is what I desire that our representatives should tell them. It is the interest of India, it is the interest of England— it is really the true interest of both countries which will be served by the grant of self-government (loud applause).

If under ordinary circumstances, this deputation is necessary, I say it is rendered more necessary now, that the Anglo-Indian agitation has succeeded in starting a new association in England under the name of the Indo-British association, Gentlemen, I must at once tell you that the name is a misnomer. There is nothing 'Indo' in that association, except this, that there are members belonging to that association who have been benefited largely by India (hear, hear) that is the only Indo about this association. There are no Indians but there are members who have lived here amongst us—I do not desire to use any harsh language—who have been profited greatly (laughter). We are told, we should be everlastingly grateful to these people for coming over here all the way and putting lots of money into their pockets and leaving us to our fate. Well, gentlemen, these are men who represent the 'Indo part of that association (laughter).

I tell you gentlemen, there is nothing British about them either (laughter). I cannot understand any association which has anything British in it which stands up against the legitimate aspirations of the people of a country (hear, hear). I refuse to believe that England has sunk so low to-day that her sons will form themselves into an association for the express purpose of crushing the legitimate aspirations of the people of India (hear, hear). Therefore, gentlemen, there is nothing "Indo" and nothing really "British" in this association which was started expressly, as I say, to oppose all reforms, to put down a whole people, so that their aspirations—their just aspirations, may be crushed for ever. So, gentlemen, if this deputation was necessary under normal circumstances, it has become absolutely necessary for our representatives to go to England to expose the vagaries of this association. If they have fed the British public with falsehood after falsehood, surely it is necessary for our representatives to meet them and expose the falsity of their utterances. Our representatives will be able to convince the British public that the grant of Home Rule is no longer a matter of gift (hear, hear). It is no longer a matter of beneficence but it is a matter of necessity which must be accomplished immediately (cheers).

They talk of progressive stages now. I say if you had started teaching the people the art of governing themselves 30 years ago, if you granted half a boon or even quarter of a boon at that time and went on granting more and more why, by to-day we would have had complete self-government in this country (hear, hear.) You have not done that. We have waited and waited and our patience is exhausted (hear, hear). Our faith in the man on the spot is gone (hear, hear) and nothing that you can do now, no honied words of beneficence, no eloquent speech of England's duty, no promise, no assurance will ever give us back that faith which you have crushed; (cheers)—that hope which you have killed (loud cheers).

What is our duty? Our duty is clear. We must depend on ourselves (hear, hear.) We must tell our own people to get ready for this great constitutional fight. It has been going on for the last 30 years but the time has come when its vigour must be doubled. We must put more energy into it, we must go on, fighting here in this country till we get what we demand. And in the meantime our representatives must go to England and acquaint the people there with the true state of affairs.—We want no favour. We have ceased to rely on beneficence or generosity. What we want is our legitimate rights. And who in this world has got the power of denying that which is ours, to claim, and to deprive us of that which is undoubtedly our right? (Loud cheers).

PRIMIERS APPEAL

Under the Presidency of Mr. Chakravarthy a largely attended meeting of the citizens of Calcutta was held in April 1918, when Mr. C. R. Das spoke :—

Mr. Chairman and gentlemen,—the resolution which has been entrusted to me is in these words (Mr. Das read the resolution). It is hardly necessary to commend this resolution to your acceptance by any lengthy speech. The resolution speaks for itself. It is only because I have heard of objections in some quarters that I have to say a few words in support of the resolution. There are people amongst us who think that it is not gracious at this time, in the face of the great danger which besets us, to trouble the Government by asking for political rights and privileges. Gentlemen, it is for the very success of the measure that I am asking the Government to consider the resolution. My answer to those critics is this : Do you think that a country where the people have been fighting for political rights for so many years and where every time their petitions and prayers have been rejected with scorn, do you think that in such a country you will get a very large army in Bengal to come forward unless you can create among them an enthusiasm, unless you can make them feel that they are fighting their own battle (hear, hear). Is it reasonable to ask the people of this country to join the army when you have made it impossible for them to feel that this is their country, when you have made it impossible for them to feel that empire you speak of is their empire? Have they any share in that empire? Is it possible for the people of this country under these circumstances to respond to the call which you have made to-day? After all, what are we asking for—is it an unreasonable request to make to the Government—here are these young men, members of many families of Bengal, whom you have interned, kept under imprisonment and in custody—is it so much unreasonable to ask Government now, in the face of a great danger, which threatens you and which threatens us, also, to release them and make them feel that after all it is their country, that there is a Government which feel for them (hear, hear)—that they have a Government also which care for their rights and privileges—is it an unreasonable request at this juncture to ask the Government to consider this resolution? Call .to arms has been sounded—it is our duty—it is the duty of every one of us to respond to that call; and I do say this, because I feel it my duty to tell the Government, at this juncture that in order that that response may be real—in order that that response may be fruitful that you ought to consider the position of these prisoners who are detained in jail and kept in custody without trial. I am not raising the question as to whether they are innocent or guilty,—let that question wait till the danger is over, I am asking the Government to release them, so that they may respond to this call to arms. With these people interned, do you think you can get thousands and tens of thousands in the army in this country? Release them. What army do you want, which Bengal cannot furnish? I take upon myself to give up my profession for six months (loud cheers) and go over the whole of this country asking the people to join the army in their thousands (cheers). I ask the Government to make it possible for us to raise this army. Gentlemen, when I think of our present position, while the danger is before us, and the attitude and the relation, if I may call it, between the Government, I mean the Bureaucracy, on the one hand, and the people on the other, I must confess, I look upon this as a tragedy. The Bureaucracy suspects the people.—Often and often have we told them, we have cried ourselves hoarse—and I repeat this again—I know these people—I have defended their cases—there is not one among the revolutionaries who wants to bring a foreign power in this country—be that foreign power Germany or Japan. I am prepared to prove it, if there is an enquiry—a proper enquiry by impartial men. But all those requests have fallen on deaf ears, Why? Because the Government distrusts the people. The result is they misunderstand us and misinterpret our statements and utterances. In the same way, we, the people mistrust them because they mistrust us. (hear, hear). I am free to confess that we very often misunderstand their declarations and mistrust them unjustly but the fact that we misunderstand each other is there, and I say it is a tragedy. I can assure the Government that I can prove it to demonstration, to whatever political party an individual in this country may belong, there is not one man in Bengal, who really desires that the English people should lose all connection with India and that some other foreign power should be brought here (loud cheers and hear, hear.) You do not believe that. We want to justify ourselves and want to become ourselves. We want to feel that this country really belongs to us—we want to feel that we are a nation—that we have got our specialities. We want to give expression to our ideals and we want to stand side by side with the different nations of the world and we do believe that with the English connection, it would be easier for us to do so than if we tried to make the English connection cease. That is the real attitude of the people. But the pity is, they will not believe us, with the result that whatever they say on many occasions, we do not believe. That is why I think it is a tragedy. I appeal to the Government again to come forward. The Prime Minister has sounded the call to arms. It is not only a call to arms but it is a call to duty (hear,

hear). We are here prepared to discharge our duty. Do you do your duty, in the same spirit—come forward and forget your racial prejudices, forget your sense of prestige.—Stand side by side with us.—Hold us by your hands and you will find between the two of us we will raise such an army in Bengal which will beat back all foreign aggression (loud cheers.) If the thing were possible, I say to the Government again, if you really think you can raise a large army in this country, if you can show us that it is probable, though I am a Nationalist, I say, that I am prepared to postpone our struggle for political privileges till the war is over. If it were possible, do it by any means. Call for any sacrifice and the people of Bengal will not be slow to respond to that. If in the face of this great danger, I ask you to release the political prisoners, it is because I feel that if you do that, that which you want will be secured. If you think you can secure what you want without releasing the political prisoners, do so. You will not find me slow to do my part of the duty (cheers.) I am prepared to wait if I see that the Government with our help can raise a large army in Bengal to-day to face a great danger—if I see that and if I find that such a course is likely to succeed, I am prepared to wait till the war is over for the fulfilment of those broken pledges. I will be prepared to wait and dream of to-morrow, of the future, when our ambitions will be satisfied—and satisfied they must be—I will forget the history of broken pledges, of dead hopes and crushed aspirations. I will wait in silence and in patience. Do make it possible. Call for any sacrifice and here we are at your service. We will wait till the war is over.—We will look forward to a later date for the fulfilment of broken pledges and the resurrection of our dead hopes and our crushed aspirations, (loud cheers.)

SELF-GOVERNMENT

Mr. C. R. Das spoke—On the third day's session of the Congress held in Calcutta in 1917.

Madam President, Ladies and Gentlemen, I have the honour to support the resolution which has been placed before you. Brother delegates, at the very outset I desire to refer to the song to which you have just listened; it is a song of the glory and victory of India. We stand here to-day on this platform for the glory and victory of India. (Cheers) and I urge you that amidst the many discussions which have taken place on the form of the resolution, you should not forget the essential idea which runs through it and which stands behind it. It is a resolution which has for its object the growth and the development of the great Indian nation. We are all agreed about that. The question is how to bring that about. Gentlemen, the Bengal ideal has been presented to you to-day by my friend, Babu Bipin Chandra Pal. I accept that ideal and if I thought that there was anything in this resolution which was inconsistent with that ideal, I should not have supported it. I do not think there is anything in this resolution which goes against the ideal which Bengal has unanimously declared by its resolution at the Bengal Provincial Conference. What is that ideal? That ideal is firstly, Provincial Autonomy *viz.*, that the Government of India must have its sphere demarcated, its functions defined; all other functions should belong to the Provincial governments of the particular province. Gentlemen, is that an ideal which is foreign to that resolution? I ask you to look into it carefully. I find within it a careful demarcation of the sphere of the Government of India and those of the Provincial governments. Therefore, so far as that ideal is concerned I do not think that this is at all inconsistent with the resolution which I have the honour to support. Now gentlemen, what is the next point in the ideal of Bengal? And that is: that the functions of the Executive Government must be made subordinate to the Legislative Council which would represent the wishes of the people of the particular province. Now is there anything in this resolution which goes against that? It may be that Bengal has provided for that in one particular way and in this resolution you have provided for that in another way, but so far as the ideal is concerned, I say that there is absolutely no difference between that of Bengal and that which is shadowed in this resolution (Hear, hear.) You say in this resolution that the power of the purse should be in the hands of the Legislature. Now, gentlemen, just pause for one moment to think what that

8

means. Let us take it that your scheme is accepted by the Government. What does that mean? That means that the Executive must be obedient to the Legislature. If they do not obey the commands of the Legislature, the Legislature will say we stop the supplies. It may be said that the British Parliament will never grant you that; but are we considering that at present? When they make a definite pronouncement as to what they are willing to give us, it will be time then to meet again and formulate a definite scheme as to the way in which that ideal may be given effect to. But the time has not come to discuss about it, because I am afraid in the discussion of it, the main ideal may get lost and I am most anxious to keep up that ideal before you. But whatever happens to the drafting of this resolution, the matter of drafting may be corrected,—I hope, gentlemen, that whatever happens, you will stick to this; that the time has come when the British Parliament must make up its mind to transfer the powers from the hands of the Bureaucracy to the people of this country. (Loud Cheers). We have had enough of the Bureaucracy in this country. We have suffered and groaned under the misrule of 150 years and not one day is to be lost in declaring our will and to see that our wishes are given effect to—that the powers which are in the hands of the Bureaucracy to-day are transferred to the people of the country. (Cheers). Now, gentlemen, having regard to that ideal, I must say that I do not see any inconsistency between what we want in Bengal and that which is put forward in the resolution. But my revered friend, Mr. Tilak said that this scheme is very much better than the Bengal scheme or any other scheme. I am speaking of Provincial Governments—of the scheme which relates to the ideal of the Provincial Governments and I do not see any difference there. Mr. Tilak thinks it is not wise to ask too much. I ask him to read the resolution again and he will find in it that it does not claim one item less than the Bengal scheme—not one item less. It claims the whole thing—it claims perfect responsible government for India. I do not understand the power over the purse to mean anything less than that. Without saying perfect responsible government for the provinces as well as for the central government, you may convey the same idea by saying: "I do not care what you do but give me the power over the purse. But if you give me the power over the purse I can have my own way. You, the executive, you say you will not obey my command but I will stop your supplies. Where are you then? You will have to obey my command." And if they obey your command what is the good of saying that we have not asked for Responsible Government? You have asked in an indirect manner, but as effectively as we have done in Bengal. You have asked not only for full responsible government for the provinces but also for the central government. Now it may be, that this ought to be put in another shape, the words may have to be changed, for this scheme does not pretend to be a perfect or an exact one.

I agree with my friend Mr. Jinnah who said: let the Government come out with a definite pronouncement—the government declaration is vague—let the government come out with its declaration—a definite pronouncement as to what they are willing to give. It will be time then to sit over this resolution again, to consider what words are to be used and what words to reject or what new words are to be put in. I think we have been fighting unnecessarily. We are all agreed as to the great ideal. Let us gather strength to fight for it—let us fight for it with all our might and let us not rest content till the whole thing is granted to us (Hear, hear), *viz.*, Responsible Government in the Provinces, responsible Government in Imperial matters—till the whole of the Government is put into the hands of the peeple. I rely on no dictum of politicians—I rely upon my natural right (Cheers). I do not care what the constitution of England or the constitution of Switzerland or that of Australia is (Cheers). I want to build my own constitution. I want the power to build my own constitution in a way which is suited to this country and which afterwards will be referred to as the great Indian constitution (Loud cheers). That is what we want and that is what we must have. Do not engage in endless discussion in the meantime. Gather all your strength and say with one voice all over India, in every village, in every town, in provincial gatherings and in this Congress that nothing less than the transference of the Governmental powers into the hands of the people will satisfy us. It is our natural right, it is the birthright of every individual to live and to grow (Hear, hear). It is the natural right of every nation to live and to grow according to its nature. (Loud cheers). We demand that right—that right has been unjustly withheld from us—by excuses and pretences—by subterfuges—we have discovered that. We were sleeping, but by God's grace, we are awake and we claim our natural right, (Prolonged cheers).

THE GREAT TRANSFORMATION.

A meeting held at Chittagong under the auspices of the local Home Rule League on the 12th June 1918, under the presidency of Babu Jatra Mohan Sen, when Mr. C. R. Das delivered the following speech :—

Mr. Chairman and gentlemen,—I thank you heartily for the many kind words with which your distinguished Chairman has introduced me to you this evening and for the kindness with which you have received me. When I set out for Chittagong I made up my mind to place before the people of Chittagong my views and the views of our friends in Calcutta on many of the important topics of the day. I am afraid I shall not be able to do so as fully as I had intended after a long day's work in Court. But I shall try to place before you in short the thoughts which are agitating the minds of our friends in Calcutta, I mean those who have worked with us the whole of last year and for many years before that in support of the cause of this country.

THE QUESTION OF THE HOUR

Gentlemen, I need hardly tell you that the most important question of the hour is the question of self-government. Upon the solution of this question depends the solution of many other questions, upon which again depend the full development of our nationality and if for the whole of last year we have been putting forth our best energies and our earnest efforts in the cause of Home Rule or self-government it is because we feel—I feel and many of my friends feel—that unless and until we have the government of this country in our own hands it is impossible to carry on the work of nation building. (Hear, Hear). Gentlemen, we could afford to be idle in the past when we hoped that the Government would do everything for us. But now after 150 years of British rule, where do we find ourselves? If you consider our position, the actual realities of our position to-day after 150 years of British rule, you will at once see that we are in a hopeless condition.

HOW DO WE STAND?

What have we got which we can call our own? If the enemy knocks at our door have we got strength to fight him? Have we got the weapons of warfare? Have we got even a lathi with which we can defend our hearths and homes?—No. (Cheers) Have we got money?—No. (Cheers) Are the people, the vast majority of the people of Bengal educated?—No. One hundred and fifty years of British rule have passed by without conferring real education on the people of this country. You need not enquire into the causes. I am only trying to give you a picture of the helplessness of our position to-day. We have not got anything—we have not got money, we have not got arms, we have not got education. Well, an analysis of our position to-day will tell you more eloquently than any speaker can that, the only solution of this question is self-government. The very objections which are urged against the granting of self-government are to my mind good reasons for granting home rule to this country (Cheers). It is said that we do not deserve Self-Government because the people of this country are not educated. My answer to that is why have they remained uneducated so long? In other countries education has been introduced and carried far within a period of 20 years or 25 years—in some countries in less than that. But why is it or how is it that within the last 150 years of British rule—the bureaucratic government in the country has not succeeded in educating the people of this country? Why is it so? It is not necessary for them. It is not necessary for the bureaucracy to do that, but it is necessary for the people of this country. It is necessary for the development of our race. It is necessary for the very existence of our notionality. Now, if you say that we are not fit for self-government because we are uneducated, I say that is the very reason why you ought to give us Home Rule, because if you do so we will succeed in educating the vast majority of our countrymen in 20 year's time (Cheers).

DO WE WANT AN OLIGARCHY?

Now, they say, well, it is only a few of you educated people who will exercise the franchise, How can you represent the country? You will be only an oligarchy. The Government, instead of being in the hands of the bureaucracy, will be transferred into the hands of an oligarchy—of another bureaucracy. My answer to that is that we do not want that. I ask you particularly to consider that question, gentlemen, and to realise its importance. My answer to them is that we do not want it. We want the franchise to be extended far and wide—we want our ryots and our cultivators to enjoy that franchise. We want them to exercise their franchise. It is against our self-interest but we want that it should be done because after all the difference between those who are against the granting of Home Rule to this country and ourselves is this: bureaucracy is against it because the granting of Home Rule means death to the bureaucracy. The Europeans, the Anglo-Indian merchants in Calcutta are against it because it is against their interest, because they thrive well under the protecting shelter of this bureaucracy. Our personal interest also lies in not getting the franchise extended all over the country —but rather in keeping it confined within the educated community, an insignificant portion of the Mahomedan community and an equally insignificant portion of the Hindu community, a few Brahmins, Baidyas and Kayesthas. If you grant franchise to all the people of this country where shall we be? In saying this I remember a conversation I had with an old friend of mine who shall be nameless. This gentleman said to me, well, if you get Home Rule, what does it mean? It means that the common people of this country will have a voice—it means they will have power and we, Brahmins, Baidyas and Kayesthas, where shall we go? I said to him in answer that they will go to a very hot place where they deserve to go. Gentlemen, I want you to realise this.

WHAT ARE WE FIGHTING FOR?

Gentlemen, we are not fighting for our narrow sordid self-interest—we are not fighting for the interest of to-day—we are not fighting for the betterment of myself or yourselves—of the present generation or of the educated community. If there are any selfish ideals pursued by any portion of our community, I stand dissociated from them and I say I take my stand on this and nothing more—it does not matter what happens to me—it does not matter what happens to the present generation—it does not matter what happens to the educated community of to-day, but what matters with me is the development of the nation (Cheers.) I look forward to the time when the Bengalee nation will rise and stand in all its glory. I do not care whether I am alive or dead at that moment (Loud Cheers)—whether my children will be living then or not—but the time will come when by God's grace, Bengalees as a nation will make themselves felt and will stand in all their strength and face the world. That is the ideal which appeals to me every moment of my life. I feel within myself that that is my appointed task. I shall devote all that I hold dear to the service of that cause and—if I die in that attempt—what then ? "Fail we alone"? —if I die in this work, I believe I shall be born in this country again and again, live for it, hope for it, work for it with all the energy of my life and with all the love of my nature, till I see the fulfilment of my hope and the realisation of this ideal (Loud Cheers).

SHALL WE FOLLOW A LEADER OF YESTERDAY EVEN WHEN HE IS WRONG

Gentlemen, when we started this agitation—basing it on the ideal to which I have just referred —ever since then we have been living under a cross fire. The bureaucracy has been against us, as it is natural they would be against us, as it is natural they should be against us. But I am sorry to say that along with these there is a party of Bengalees in Calcutta who also have set themselves against the fulfilment of this noble ideal. When I read the criticisms which appear in the *Statesman* or the *Englishman* I feel glad because I know that we have succeeded in exposing the illogical position which they take. But when I read similar things in the

Bengalee, I assure you, I feel a great pain in my heart. I cannot understand it. Is this ideal to be pursued from the consideration of purely personal question? We have been told that the leaders of yesterday are the only people who can lead us. I do not deny their claim to lead. But I am not one of those who would follow a leader simply because he was a leader yesterday. I want him to lead. Anybody who leads the real politics of the country at the present time is a man whom I honour and I am prepared to bow down and take the dust of his feet. But if a man comes to me and says : look here you will have to do this—it does not matter what the people of Bengal want—I am the leader of Bengal—this has been done by me—it has got to be supported—well, my answer to him is : "thou imposter !" No one has got that right. We stand or fall as we pursue or desist from the popular cause. I am nothing. No leader is anything. The strength belongs to the nation whose representative I am, whose representative every one of us may become. It is not my own strength. It is the peoples' strength. Take your stand on that and we will worship you as a leader, as a martyr, as anything which you can claim but fall short of that ideal once by a hair's breadth, your claim is no longer to be recognised. If I have expressed myself strongly, believe me, gentlemen, it is because I have felt deeply—I feel, I have been stabbed to the heart by this attitude—this contempt of public opinion.

WAS THERE AN UNDERTAKING?

Now, gentlemen, you all know that we are expecting a scheme of self-government from the British Parliament. What that scheme is I do not know. No one has got the right to know but we are expecting some scheme. We heard that Mr. Montagu had shown or talked about the outline of that scheme to some Indian leaders—Mr. Surendranath Banerjea of Bengal, Pundit Madan Mohan Malaviya of the U. P. and Mr. Shastri of Madras and certain other gentlemen. I do not know if it is true but I suspect it is. We are also told—it is not admitted—we are told that some of these gentlemen had given a promise to the Secretary of State that they would get the people of this country to accept that scheme. I am not saying that this is admitted but that is what I have heard.

THE CONFIDENTAL LETTER.

Now what do we find after that? A few days after Mr. Montagu's departure, a confidental letter over the signature of Babu Satyananda Bose was circulated and anybody who reads that letter will see that the attempt is to give up what was decided in the Bengal Provincial Conference for all Bengal, —to give it up, and to take whatever is offered to us by the Secretary of State! Why was that circular issued? Was it only Mr. Satyananda Bose who circulated this or was there a party behind it? We know Mr. Satyananda Bose is a follower of

Mr. Surendranath Banerjea. Was it the attempt of only Mr, Satyananda Bose or was it a subtle attempt made in the dark to throw out to the people the suggestion that they ought to be satisfied with anything which it may please Mr. Montagu to give, to prepare the ground for the acceptance of Mr. Montagu's scheme? After that we heard that a special session of the Congress would be held in Bombay.

THE CONGRESS COMMITTEE'S CIRCULAR

It is after that that the secretaries of the Provincial Congress Committee wrote this letter:

> " Dear Sir,—It appears that the Secretary of State for India will very soon make his announcement about the proposed Reforms. It is in contemplation to hold a special session of the Congress and of the Provincial Conference after the announcement. We have a duty to perform. The future of our country for at least a generation will depend upon the nature of the Reforms. You will therefore keep yourselves ready to hold public meetings, to attend the Congress (wherever held) and the Conference in very large numbers and to fearlessly criticise the proposals if they fall short of our ideal. We must make a united stand and see that they meet our legitimate aspirators. Yours faithfully,—*I. B. Sen, Bejoy Krishna Bose, Secys.*

Now, gentlemen, you have heard the whole of this letter. Do you think there is anything objectionable in this letter? What does the letter say? It says merely that Mr. Montagu is going to make his pronouncement and that we have to watch, if it falls short of our ideal and our legitimate aspirations and if so we ought to fight against it, we ought to attend in large numbers, the special session of the Congress and conference to show a united front, and to criticise the scheme fearlessly. Now, is there anything in this to which any Nationalist, any person who has the good of his country at heart can take the slightest objection?

THE 'BENGALEE'S PATHOS

I will read out to you what the *Bengalee* says, Unfortunately we cannot dissociate the Editor of the *Bengalee* from the paper. Otherwise I would have cast it into the waste-paper basket and would not have thought about it. This is what the *Bengalee* writes in its editorial of June 6th;—

> "We confess that we have read the above with pain and regret, though not with surprise, for in a recent article, we pretty clearly indicated the constitution and the policy of the present Bengal Provincial Congress Committee. The old leaders are the men of yesterday and they of course should have no voice in the deliberation of the *New India* which they have helped to build up. For we are always wiser than our fathers, and to acknowledge our indebtedness to them is to belittle our own

importance which must always be a prime consideration. There is only one little risk which their policy involves and they may as well be reminded of it thus early, *viz*, that they may be paid back in their own coins and with compound interest by those who come after them."

What is there in this innocent letter to call for this personal and vehement attack? Are we to be condemned because we are asking the people of this country to watch the pronouncement of the Secretary of State? We are asking the people of this country to examine it and if it falls short of popular demands to criticise it, fearlessly and to hold meetings and to attend those meetings in large numbers. "Large numbers" is italicised by the *Bengalee*. It is a crime, a new crime to hold meetings where "large numbers" attend. It used not to be so in the past but it has become a crime now! I will go on reading another passage from this article:—

THE REALLY GREAT DANGER

"Let us now pass on to the consideration of the circular. The tone is pessimistic. It is even worse: it is that of the alarmist who raises the signal note of warning, as if we were on the eve of a great danger."

Well, gentlemen, if I am to tell you the truth, I admit that I suspect we are on the eve of a great danger and that grave danger is the acceptance of a system of self-government which will not give us the reality, which will give us self-government in name but not in fact. It is the duty of every Nationalist to raise that alarm. It does no harm to watch, even suspiciously watch what it is and if it does not satisfy the people of this country, to reject it, to say that we do not want it,—Take it back.

> "Our countrymen are asked to be ready to fearlessly criticise the proposals, if they fall short of our ideal."

Very wrong indeed! Now mark what follows:—

> "Brave words indeed coming with special aptness from some of those who ran away as fast as their legs could carry them when the Police broke up the Barisal Conference."

That is worthy of the leader of the Bengalee nation! To circulate—this falsehood! It may be within the recollection of many of you (Jatra Mohan Babu nods his head)—it is within the recollection of our distinguished Chairman—this falsehood originated in Colootolla in the year 1906 or 1907. The falsity of this was demonstrated then and now in the year of grace, 1918, we find the truthful Editor of the *Bengalee* newspaper referring to that lie and putting forward that lie as an argument against the popular party.

> "We are told that we must fearlessly criticise the proposals, if they fall short of our ideal. But if they do not, what then?"

Well then, we accept it (Laughter). What is there to say about it? Then it goes on to say:

> "The circular assumes that Mr. Montagu's proposals are bound to be unsatisfactory and that they will mean little or nothing."

Where does the Circular assume that? The Circular merely asserts that if it is, it is our bounden duty to protest against that. Nothing more.

I need not read the rest of it. There is another passage which however I must read to you:

> "Why then sound the tocsin of alarm and seek to create a prejudice for which so far as there is no warrant and against which there is a strong body of presumptive evidence. Why talk of fearless criticism and united front"?

This comes from Mr. Surendranath Banerjea! Surely we are fallen on evil times!

THE OLD "LEADER'S ADVICE TO THE PEOPLE."

Then our editor goes on to say:

> "If they are satisfactory they should be welcomed; if they are partly satisfactory they should be welcomed to that extent."

(Never)

And why?

> "For the British public would then feel inclined to drop them altogether."

To drop them altogether! Now, gentlemen, you have seen what that article is. The letter which was written by the Secretaries of the Provincial

Congress Committee is merely put forward as an excuse. What is put forward before the people of Bengal is this; if it is satisfactory, of course, we should accept it. If not? In the article which appeared the next day, he made his position clearer. He said. the difficulty is this: The Europeans are clamouring against it—the Indo-European Association in England is fighting against it—and if you, the people of Bengal say that you do not want it, why the British people will say 'then drop it altogether.' My answer to that is: let it be dropped if it is not satisfactory. Mr. Surendranath Banerjea admits it in this writing—let me quote his exact words:

> "We quite admit that there have been many paper announcements in the past: and it is only too true that the pages of Anglo-Indian history are strewn broadcast with the fragments of broken pledges."

Let it be another fragment of broken pledge; but let not the people of Bengal consent to that! If their position is this: we will give you this and no further; let them give what they choose; but is it for us to say what little of self-government you choose to give us is amply sufficient for us at the present day? I venture to think that you will not accept such a proposition as that (No, no). We want self-government for a purpose. We do not want that self-government which some people brought up in European politics want—we do not want simply a weapon to fight against the bureaucracy—we have got tired of that and we say for God's sake, let us have peace in Bengal. (cheers) Let us have some sort of self-government which will enable us to look after the agricultural, industrial interests of the country, and to take up the work of education and sanitation which will enable us to work for the real good of the country without being obstructed at every step. That is why we want a change in the system of Government (cheers).

"BENGALEE'S" WRITINGS BEFORE MR. BANNERJEA WENT TO DELHI.

Now, gentlemen, supposing Mr. Montagu says you can't get all that, take a little, just a little, a pinch. My position is this: I do not know what others will say. I hope the people of this country will have the courage to say: we want none of it, take it back: if we are to be slaves of the bureaucracy, if all our activities in every direction are to be controlled, and it may be, stifled at the sweet will and pleasure of the bureaucracy, we want none of it. Take it back to England (cheers). We do not want it here. We want courage to say that, I admit. But what right have you to ask for Home Rule if you cannot have the courage to say that —if you cannot have the courage to say to the Government that we don't want it: it will not serve our purpose: What is the good of giving something to the people which they do not want. Now, gentlemen, that I am right in taking this position I shall try to show to you, if you will bear with me—(go on) from one or two extracts from the "Bengalee" newspaper, before a change came over the spirit of its dreams. I will read to you just two or three extracts from the "Bengalee"—not after March when the editor went to Delhi but before that in November and December, 1917. I quote from the "Bengalee" of November 2nd 1917 :—

> "Mr. Montagu will not be deceived by these tactics (of the anti-Congress-League party). He will know how to appraise them at their proper value. The British Cabinet consisting of politicians of the type of Lord Curzon and Lord Milner have decided that India is to have responsible government and that a substantial advance is to be made in that direction as soon as possible. There is no going back upon this announcement. It must be accepted as a settled policy, from which there can be no departure. Mr. Montagu is coming out to discuss the details and how best this policy can be carried out. It is no use saying "we don't want responsible government; we are not fit for it."

This was Mr. Surendranath Banerjea on November 2nd 1917. He says :—

> "Those who breathe a word against it in this crisis of our national evolution are traitors to their country and their God."

This was Mr. Surendranath Banerjea on November 2nd, 1917. On 3rd November, 1917, the mood still continues:

> "We want responsible government in full measure in connection with the Provincial Branches of administration, leaving untouched the Departments under the control of the Government of India in regard to which the Congress scheme should apply."

Therefore what he wanted is responsible government in full measure in connection with the provincial branches. On the 11th November, the "Bengalee" writes:

> "In Bengal the feeling is—and we think that Bengal reflects the feeling of all India in this matter—that a full measure of provincial autonomy should be at once given with the reform of the Imperial Legistative Couucil of the India office as recommended by the Congress and the Muslim League. Nothing short of this will satisfy educated India."

This was Mr. Surendranath Banerjea on November 11th. If he is a leader of yesterday, let him remain true to that leadership (Hear, hear). As for myself, standing on this platform to-day, I make a solemn promise to follow this leader if he remains true to what he was yesterday (cheers). I shall follow what Mr. Surendranath Banerjea said on November 11th, 1917 *viz*., that nothing short of this will satisfy educated India (loud cheers). Then on the 21st. November, he repeats the same ideal:

> "Courage is the first and last quality of real statesmanship. It was the crowning quality of Akbar, the greatest ruler that ever adorned a throne. Let our rulers take courage in both hands and great will be their reward."

Courage is the first and last quality of real statesmanship! How have the mighty fallen!

NO SHAMS, NO DELUSIONS SAID MR. BANERJEA OF 1917.

He follows that up by saying on November 22nd:

> "There must be no shams or shows or delusions. We have had too much of this commodity in the past.

No shams, no delusions. I follow the noble words of Mr. Surendranath Banerjea. I love them so much that I am prepared to follow his teachings. But if the Surendranath Banerjea of to-day does not follow the S. N. Banerjea of yesterday is it my fault that I cannot follow him? (laughter) I adore the Surendranath Banerjea of yesterday, but if he cannot remain true to his trust I cannot be false to my faith. Hear the leader of yesterday again:

> "The Minto-Morley scheme, if it was not a dead failure, did not satisfy popular aspirations and was behind the growing requirements of the times. We hope the mistakes will not be repeated in the coming constitutional changes Provincial autonomy must be the basis of the

> reforms, not an emasculated, half-hearted, system of Provincial self-government."

Noble words again and I repeat them and I follow them.

> "but in full measure with a full share of responsibility. The time for half-measures is past and gone."

Then in the same article he goes on to say:

> "The counsels of caution are often the counsels of timidity."

Mark these words, gentlemen. Then he says:

> "If the Government will not make over the whole of the provincial administration to a popular Ministry responsible to a popular Assembly, let them at least, entrust to them such departments, as Education, Sanitation, Local Self-government, Police, etc."

Mark these words again. He includes the Police but I was told the other day that we ought not to take the Police; it is a difficult department to administer, (laughter).

Then on the 27th of November, the "Bengalee" writes;

> "The country is rushing at a giddy pace and Lord Morley's reforms have failed to meet the exigencies of the times which cannot be satisfied by anything short of a full measure of responsible government."

Further:

> "Any scheme that does not fully provide for this and secure full autonomous power for the

provinces and falls short of the irreducible minimum put forth in the Congress-League scheme stands self-condemned and will totally fail to meet the wishes and requirements of the people and win their support."

But now he is urging the people of this country to support a scheme which may fall short of his ideal and he says even if it is not satisfactory we should accept it. Even on the 29th of November, he says:

"Any tinkering reform of a patch-work kind will not avail to meet the necessities of the situation but will rather intensify the present difficulties."

Gentlemen, I will not weary you with any more extracts but I will quote just two passages, for which I hope you will pardon me (go on, go on),

SURENDRANATH OF DECEMBER, 1917.

On December 1st, Mr. Surendranath Banerjea says:

"Nothing less will satisfy the people of India or redeem the honour of England......Real power must be given to us. No shams or delusions will satisfy us. We have had enough of them......None of that taking away with the one hand what is given with the other."

Then on the 2nd of December, he says:

"Let it be clearly understood that the Congress-League scheme represents the irreducible minimum which admits of no curtailment here or excision there and than which no more moderate demand can be conceived under the circumstances

It seems to me, gentlemen, that a scheme more moderate than the Congress League scheme can be conceived and Mr. Surendranath Banerjea of to-day has conceived that (laughter). Then on December 12th, he says:

"Too long have we been given the shadows of things—empty forms—which may please the infantile mind, but which the adolescent natio nspurns away as a child's plaything ......Not only should justice be done, but that the people should be convinced of it, ...not only should the Government be satisfied, but that the people should be convinced that a substantial measure of responsible government has been granted."

THE GREAT TRANSFORMATION.

Gentlemen, you will find similar expressions of his opinion in January and one or two in February. In March, Mr. Surendranath Banerjea went to Delhi and from that moment—well I am reminded of the "Rake's progress"—I shudder to think of the last step—I think, we the people of Bengal—we are entitled to ask for an explanation of this phenomenon. We are entitled to ask Sir Surendranath—I beg your pardon, gentlemen, I beg his pardon too—coming events cast their shadow before and I was caught in that shadow just for a moment—I think, gentlemen, we are entitled to ask Mr. Surendranath why is it that yesterday he was determined not to have any measure of self-government which was not satisfactory, which was not responsible, which was not wide in its scope and why is it that to-day in the month of June, 1918, he is of opinion that whatever scheme the Secretary of State puts forward should be accepted by the people—if it is satitfactory it should be accepted, if it is not satisfactory, even then it should be accepted because if we did not accept it, the British people might not grant anything at all. We want an explanation of this. He is the leader of Bengal—he claims that. I am free to acknowledge that claim, but we the people of Bengal who have loved him, followed him and honoured him, we who had "learnt his great language" and "caught his clear accents," we who had followed him with all the devotion of our hearts, we who had lived "in his mild and magnificent eye" for the last 30 years, are we not entitled to ask him to explain to us the inner significance the deeper meaning of this change ? (Hear hear,) It cannot be for "a handful silver," we are told, it is not for "a riband to stick in his coat." What is it then ?

WAS IT TOUCH OF HAND OR TURN OF HEAD ?

Was there anything in the atmosphere of Delhi which brought about this change—was it something said, something done?—was it touch of hand or turn of head? What was it? Was it the growing wisdom of old age? Surely some explanation is due from him to the people of Bengal and as for his reasons, I have told you and I repeat: as long as I shall live I shall repeat that whether the people of England are willing or not willing to grant us any reform, that will not induce me to accept it unless it recognises my natural right—a real scheme of reform means the recognition of the natural rights of the people of this country (Loud cheers) I claim no favour. I stand on my right.

WE STAND ON OUR RIGHTS

What rights can the British people give me if I have not the claim within myself? Can man create rights? They can only recognise the rights which I have within me, the rights which belong to me, the rights which are given to me by God and rights which no man can take away. Unless you can satisfy that, unless you can make good that position, neither the British Parliament, nor all the Parliaments of the world will be able to confer on you things which do not belong to you. Strive for the thing which belongs to you. Say to them manfully, "this is my right" and prove that assertion by the voice of the people, the united voice of the nation (cheers). Prove that assertion and when you have done that, is there any power in this world which can say, you will not have that which belongs to you (cheers). They can only keep it from you as long as you do not realise that it is yours.' That which you realise as your own cannot be taken away from you. The moment you realise this is your own, that moment that right will have to be recognised and not a moment sooner. No half-measures will create that, no tinkering scheme of reforms has ever made a nation in the past and will never make a nation in the future. Is it not Mr. Surendranath Banerjea who has repeated times without number that nations are by themselves made (Loud Cheers)?

THD WISDOM OF THE LEADER OF YESTERDAY

We have to make ourselves. Is this the way? This way which Mr. Surendranath Banerjea is now recommending, is this the way to make a nation? It is a critical period in our political history: there was no crisis in the history of India from the earliest times down to the present which was more critical than this and at this critical time for a leader of our people to say 'give us what little you think wise, we, the people of this country will accept it.' -Is it politics? Is it wisdom? Or is it madness? Surely an explanation is due to the people.

Well, gentlemen, take this to your heart to-day and make a solemn vow that if you are fit for self-gevernment, you have got to demonstrate that. No words ever produced or created rights. Enactments are nothing. They simply recognise rights which exist. The rights belong to you if you only realise the position—they are not yours, if you hesitate (cheers). If you hesitate, you are lost. If you are afraid to realise that you have rights you are not fit for self-government. The rights of nationality were never granted to a nation of cowards (hear, hear).

I thank you again, gentlemen, for listening to me patiently. I had many things more to say and if I find another opportunity I shall again address you (cheers).

THE GREAT DENIAL

At Chittagong on the 17th June 1918, under the auspices of the local Home Rule League, a meeting was held under the presidency of Babu Jatra Mohan Sen, when Mr. C. R. Das delivered the following speech :—

Mr. Chairman and gentlemen, I wish you had not insisted on my speaking to-night as I am anxious not to spoil the effect of the brilliant address (of the Hon. Mr. Fazlul Huq) to which you have just listened (go on, go on). If I rise to respond to the call from the Chairman, I confess it is not without some hesitation. Gentlemen, Mr. Huq has dealt with the question of Home Rule from many points of view, with considerable force and with great eloquence. I desire to say that I am in complete agreement with everything that has fallen from him. (Cheers).

You will, however, permit me to-night to tell you a story—the story of the great denial. The other day our distinguished Chairman said that we are in the midst of a great crisis. I also said that the present crisis of India is greater and more serious than any in her history. But to-day I will tell you the story of the great denial. As a preface to my story I shall ask you to recall to your mind the principal incidents of our national history under British Rule. More than a century and a half have passed by and at the end of it we find that the people of Bengal, the vast majority of them at any rate, are not educated and this want of education is put forward by the authorities as an argument against Home Rule. I have given this anwer before and I repeat it again—if they are not educated, whose fault is it? What have the authorities been doing here for the last 150 years if they have not succeeded in educating the people of this country? What excuse is there for this failure? Is there a national government anywhere in the history of civilization, which after it took up the work of education, did not finish and complete it within, say, 30 years? (Hear, hear). Do you doubt for a moment that if we get self-government now, we will be able to educate the people of this country in another 20 years? But why has not this been done by the Government? Let the Bureaucracy answer—This is a chapter in the story of the great denial (Hear, hear).

OUR AGRICULTURE

Now, gentlemen, take the question of agriculture in this country. The Indian village-life was the envy of the world at one time. What are our villages now? How does our agriculture stand to-day? Has the Government done anything on that behalf during the last 150 years, which is at all worthy of a great nation and a great Government? (Cries of 'no,' 'no'). Yes, the answer must be 'no'. Why not? Because agriculture does not directly concern the bureaucracy of this country. It may be necessary to start a department and call it department of agriculture in the interest of the bureaucracy. that has been done—one or two colleges which are not suited to our requirements have been established. But has agriculture improved? I do not know whether in the interest of the Bureaucracy it is necessary that it should. But it is necessary for us. It is a matter of vital importance to the nation that the cultivators of Bengal should prosper and live better lives (hear, hear). It is a matter of supreme importance to those who want self-government or swaraj in this country (hear, hear). We must look forward to the whole Bengalee nation. We must work persistently, we must look forward to the day when the Bengalees as a nation, Hindus and Mahomedans, all together, will stand before the world in all the glory of nationality (cheers). I say therefore the question is of vital importance from the point of view of the nation. Who are the people of Bengal? Not we, who conduct cases in court, not those who sit as magistrates and judges. But who are they? It is those who cultivate the land—they are the real nation (cheers) and if ever this country rises—by God's grace, rise it must—and takes its place amongst the nations of the world (Loud cheers)—well, long before that, the agriculture of this country must be improved. That is one of the reasons why we want Home rule. This is another chapter in the story of the great denial (hear, hear).

OUR COMMERCE AND INDUSTRY

Now, gentlemen, what is the story of our commerce and industry? I do not desire to begin from the beginning. I will not recall to mind or help you to recall to your mind the history of the destruction of our trade and the annihilation of our industries. Let the dead past bury its dead. But what about the living? What has the Government done to encourage Commerce and Industry in recent years? It is the crying need of the hour—the peculiar circumstances of this country demand a solution of this problem. Has the bureaucracy done anything in this matter? It is the duty of every civilized government to lend a helping hand and thus encourage the growth of Commerce and Industry. Can the Bureaucracy lay its hand on its breast and say that it has fulfilled its trust? The answer must be 'no'. That is another reason why we want Home Rule, and gentlemen, that is another chapter in the story of the great denial (hear, hear).

Do you want proof? For agriculture, the Government spends only 24 lacs of rupees out of Bengal's share of land-revenue which is 1½ crores. What do the Government do with that money? The Bureaucracy says we who want Home Rule are not fit to represent the people! What has the Government done for them? They spend only 24 lacs of rupees or rather misspend it. Have any improvements been effected? That is the test. It is possible to have highly paid European agricultural officers without agricultural improvements.

That is exactly what has happened!

FIVE MILLION SOULS LOST IN FIVE YEARS

Now, gentlemen, what about sanitation? Shall I tell you the story of how the people are dying in this country for want of sanitation for the last few years? Listen to these figures.

In 1911-12—9 lacs of people died of malaria alone
In 1912-13—9·59 " " "
In 1913-14—9·65 " " "
In 1914-15—10·61 " " "
In 1915-16—10·64 " " "

So in five years we have had five million victims (Cries of Oh!) for want of sanitation in this country. Five million men in five years! More than the combined army of Great Britain and Ireland to-day! (Cries of Oh!) We have had representations and opinions of experts and a few experiments but what has really been done up to now? Are we to believe that this fell disease could not have been eradicated if the Government had taken active steps in that direction? Do you believe, gentlemen that if the government is nationalised—effectively nationalised—we cannot get rid of this disease? It is a matter of supreme importance to us, to the growing nationality of Bengal. It means that every year there is an increase in the number of deaths, it means want of strength, it means decrease of national vitality, it means that at not a very distant day we will be reduced to such a condition that it will be impossible to regenerate us. (hear, hear). I have given you only the number of people who die every year. But do we not see all over the whole country malaria-stricken people living by chance as it were—carrying on by some means or other, their miserable load of existence? The whole of Bengal is full of these people and yet what has the Government done? ('Nothing') Yes, practically nothing.

EDUCATIONAL EXPENDITURE.

Three Annas per Head per Year.

Let me give you the figures regarding education which is very interesting. The average amount spent by the Government is 85 lacs of rupees for education. The population of Bengal is 450 lacs, *i. e.*, 5 persons per rupee per year. It means three annas per head per year spent for the noble cause of education! (laughter) It means again one pice per head per month! (Shame). And we are told that England's duty in India is to spread education so that the degraded people of the country may be elevated! (laughter) And three annas per head per year is spent for this noble cause! But don't you think these are purely educational expenses. It also includes the cost of building (Laughter). It includes the cost of inspection which exceeds the pay of the teachers (Shame). You can well imagine what is left for education proper. Talk of education gentlemen? Who cares for education? Not the bureaucracy.

GOVERNMENT ENCOURAGEMENT OF COMMERCE AND INDUSTRY—MR. SWAN'S RECOMMENDATIONS.

With regard to expenditure on commerce and industry, well, you may say very little, practically nothing is spent. I will simply quote to you the observations of a member of the Indian Civil Service, Mr. J. Swan, who has written a report on the industrial condition of Bengal.

"While the industrial development of the province must depend on private enterprise I think the encouragement of Government might take a more active form than it has hitherto done."

Encouragement of the Government might take a more active form! Well, you cannot expect a member of the Civil Service to write more than that. Then again :—

"Adequate capital is particularly necessary in case of industries run by Indian capital and under Indian management owing to the reluctance of banks and of firms to give them credit."

THE REVOLUTIONARY MOVEMENT

This is what Mr. Swan writes. You may gather therefore that very little is done for industry and commerce. Now that is the position. This state of things went on for years. We were sleeping. At the end of every year we used to hold a meeting of the Congress and beyond that we had no kind of activity. But from the year 1905, there was a great activity in this country which we called the Swadeshi movement. And we find from that time the Government indulged in a series of repressive measures and I believe those repressive measures in their turn gave rise to a party in Bengal, who are described by the Government as anarchists but who are, I venture to think, not anarchists at all—they are revolutionaries. I do not for a moment suggest that the mehtods which they employ are good or ought to be encouraged but they are not anarchists. It is not that they want to do away with all Government—what they want to do is to change the system of government (hear, hear). So far as I have been able to judge the object of these socalled anarchists is not different from the object of the Congress or the Moslem League. The only difference lies in the method which they pursue. They pursue methods which are subversive of law and order whereas the Congress-League adopts methods which are legal. This is the only difference. The methods they pursue are deserving of severe condemnation but I think it is a great injustice to call them anarchists. Be that as it may —I say that after these repressive measures, one after another, in rapid succession—we have in our midst a revolutionary party in Bengal.

Now, it has been often said that we are not fit for self-government because of the existence of this revolutionary party. My answer is: I do not deny that there is a revolutionary party. I admit it and I say that no government which is not a national government will ever be able to put a stop to this revolutionary movement. What do these people want? They want freedom. They want to change the system of government. I told you just now that their object is the same as that of the Congress and the Moslem League. I go further and I say that their object—not their methods—is now recognised as legitimate by the British Cabinet. In August last year, the British Cabinet declared that some kind of responsible government should be introduced into this country. What does that mean? It means that the system of government which obtains now, which is bureaucratic, should be changed or otherwise it is an admission on the part of our masters—after all it is the British Cabinet who are our masters and not the Bureaucracy here —it is an admission on the part of our masters that a change of government, of the bureaucratic system of government is necessary for the welfare of India. I say the object of the so-called anarchists is not only the same as that of the Congress and the League but it is an object which is recognised and sanctioned by the highest authority in England. Therefore, gentlemen, I say, as I have said elsewhere, that the only way you can put a stop to this revolutionary movement is by recognising that simple fact that the people of this country—they are hungry for Freedom—should be given what they want and I say the moment you give freedom to the people, there will be an end of this revolutionary movement (hear, hear). It has been pointed out over and over again, but the Bureaucracy will not listen. Gentlemen, that is the position of affairs to-day. Our agriculture neglected, our education neglected, sanitation neglected, industry and commerce not seriously considered and along with that we have got a revolutionary movement in this country. This is the present situation and it is upon that that a memorable declaration was made by the British Cabinet in August last year. Now, gentlemen, what have we to say to that? I desire to place before you clearly what I mean: Your declaration goes one way and your action goes another way. That is the real grievance of the people of this country. Tell us, if you want, 'you are not fit for self-government, we will not give you self-government.' I can understand that position. I respect plain speaking. I am fond of plain speaking. Let the bureaucracy say in clear terms 'we cannot afford to give you responsible government. We want to have this government as bureaucratic as ever.' 'You can get a little change here and there, political lolipops with which you can amuse yourselves. But we will not give you responsible government '—let them so declare, if they like, and we will then drop this political agitation. Our difficulty is this: We believe in the words of the Declaration and in that belief we have been devising schemes, holding meetings to consider schemes of self-government and to consider what would be the best form of self-government, in this country and to help the Government with our suggestions so that the British Parliament may consider this.

HOW GOVERNMENT HAS TREATED HOME RULERS' PROPOSAL

Now, gentlemen, when things were going on in that way we had another declaration, a more memorable message from the Prime Minister, in which the Prime Minister asked our help at the time of a great crisis, asked us to avert a great danger which threatened England and which threatened India. Now what did we do under the circumstance? We held meetings again and we told the Government that at this juncture 'you must have one united India, you must create an enthusiasm in this country, real enthusiasm which will lead people to make every sacrifice for the country and for the empire' and we asked the Government to do away with the repressive measures, to release the political suspects and the political prisoners (loud cheers). The whole country regards that as an oppression. We said to the Government. Do away with that oppression: Make a definite proposal about self-government and you will have the whole country with you. You will have hundreds and thousands of soldiers fighting for you, fighting for India, fighting for the Empire—you will have the gold of the rich and the copper of the poor—every sacrifice that may be required of the people will be willingly, ungrudgingly, cheerfully made for the service of the country and for upholding the glory of the empire (cheers). How was that accepted by the bureaucracy? I must confess to a sense of hopelessness that Government paid not the slightest attention to it. Shortly after that there was the Conference at Delhi. Let me quote to you the words of His Excellency the Viceroy, words in which he pictures the great danger which threatens us:

"Germany has already thrown out into Central Asia her pioneers of intrigue, her agents of disintegration. The lesson she has learnt from the Russian Revolution that a stronger weapon than all the armaments that money can buy or science devise is the disruption of an enemy by his own internal forces."

Then later on,

"I have spoken of the cause. I have told you of the death-grip on the western front and have unfolded to you the story of German machinations in the East."

We were ready to help the Government when we were told that a great danger threatened the whole of the British Empire and India. That danger is admitted by His Excellency the Viceroy, it was suggested by the message of the Prime Minister. It was admitted and if I may have the impertinence of saying, clearly and eloquently described by His Excellency the Viceroy. But what about our suggestions? Is it not a fact that whenever we are anxious to give the bureaucracy in this country good advice, sane advice, advice which is necessary for the welfare not only of this country but of England also, the welfare of the whole empire, that advice is received with scorn and contempt? What does the Viceroy say? After describing the difficulty which threatens us, His Excellency says:

"We can, I believe, best do so (help the Amir to keep his ship straight) by showing our enemies first that India is solid as a rock."

I pause here for a moment. That must be done. It is admitted by His Excellency the Viceroy that at this juncture we must do something by which we can present to the enemy a united India, an India which is solid as a rock. How does he propose to do that? How can India be solid as a rock unless she is strong in her rights, how can anybody expect India to stand solid as a rock unless she has got the elementary rights of citizenship, unless she can say 'I am one in this world'? (Cheers). The Viceroy says :—

"We can, I belive, best do so by showing our enemies first that India is solid as a rock, and that the lambent flame of anarchical intrigue will find nothing inflammable in this country, nay, rather will be smothered and extinguished forthwith should it approach, by the deadweight of our unity of purpose."

Now, gentlemen, so far, there is nothing in the speech of His Excellency the Viceroy from which we have any reason to differ. But in the same speech His Excellency disposes of our suggestions in this way:

"But in these days of stress and strain it is idle to ask men to come together who disagree on first principles."

DO WE DISAGREE ON FIRST PRINCIPLES ?

I pause for a moment. Do we disagree—we the nationalists of India, do we disagree from the Viceroy on any question of first principles? I venture to think, not. What have we done? We have believed the Message of Hope left to us by His Majesty the King personally—we have believed that that message will be fulfilled—we have had the declaration of the British Cabinet in that behalf and we believed that Responsible Government would be introduced. We have had the message from the Prime Minister asking for our help and sympathy, asking for help in men and money. We have told the Government that in order to do this, the repressive measures must be withdrawn, political prisoners must be set free and a definite scheme of self-government must be put forward. What were we trying to do? Were we not trying to give effect to the message of the British Cabinet? Were we not giving a real response to the message of the Prime Minister? (Cheers). Why should it be said that we differ from the Viceroy on questions of first principles. What are the questions of first principles? It is statements like these which fill us with suspicion and alarm. Do they want that the King's Message will for ever remain unfulfilled and unredeemed?—That the Declaration of the British Parliament will remain a declaration and nothing but a Declaration to the end of the chapter?—Does it come to this: that whatever declaration is made the bureaucray has made up its mind not to let responsible government be introduced in this country? What difference in first principles can there be, I ask, when all our endeavours have been to give effect to the Message of the Prime Minister?

Then His Excellency goes on to say:

"While they are wrangling over those, while the house is burning, there are those who would exploit England's difficulty. I believe that these people gravely misinterpret India's attitude. I am sure that there are none here who will countenance such a policy. There are those, again, who would wish to bargain. Again I decline to believe that anyone has come to this Conference in a huckstering spirit."

IS WHAT GOVERNMENT DOING NOT BARGAINING?

There are those who would wish to bargain, that is to say, when we are suggesting to the Government in all seriousness that certain measures are necessary for carrying out the Prime Minister's Message we are told that it is bargaining, that we want to exploit England's difficulty! What is England doing now? This is a simple fact and I do not wish to conceal it. What is our interest in the war? Our only interest is our country. What is England doing now? England asks us to help her in this war. And why should we help her? If we are to help her, we must first of all feel that this country is our own country (Cheers)—that India has in fact and not in name, her rightful place in the British Empire (Loud Cheers). That is what we say. That is what great statesmen in England have said again and again. If this is your real intention, tell the people so—tell them "it is your own country, manage your own affairs and defend your own country" and you will then see what we can do (Hear, Hear). The only thing that we want is to feel that this is our country. If it is not our country, what does it matter to us? (Cheers). If it is our country it affects us; it affects our personal interests, it affects our selfish interests, it affects our future—and we are ready for any sacrifice. You say that we want to exploit England's difficulty. And if we say that England is exploiting at this time our helplessness, that would at once be condemned as unwise and unworthy. Those who wish to realise themselves, those who wish to make the people of this country realise that India is their own country, that India is a part, an integral part—not shadowy or imaginary but a real part of the British Empire—well, they are to be condemned as persons who would exploit England's difficulty (Shame). That is how the Conference was held at Delhi.

HIS EXCELLENCY THE GOVERNOR OF BENGAL'S ADVICE.

From Delhi we come to Bengal. There again we have the speech of His Excellency the Governor. His Excellency advised us—he did not command—His Excellency advised us that we should stop all political agitation at the present moment and he gave two reasons for it. One reason is this :

"Now let me give you my first reason. We have always been slow as a people, as in Great Britain and India to realise how closely the enemy keeps his eye upon us how quick he is to note our actions, indeed our very words, and what a difference it makes to his own morals whether he sees arrayed against him the serried ranks of a united people or whether he detects or thinks he detects in this part of the Empire or in that some note of dissension, some indication of lack of unity of purpose."

Therefore, do not show that you are wanting in a unity of purpose. I was thinking what His

Excellency really meant because it seems to me that we are in complete agreement with what His Excellency said. That is the very reason for which we made the suggestions. Let not the enemy think that England is not united in its purpose and that India is not prepared to take its place in the fight. That is the very reason for which we suggested that all causes which led to resentment of the psople of this country and drew them away from this united purpose should be removed—that the people of this country should be allowed to feel that India is their own country, that it is their birthright to defend their own country, that it is their right, not right alone but it is their proud privilege to fight the common enemy. His Excellency said we should do nothing so that the enemy could think that we are not united. My answer is: Make us united. It can be done with a stroke of the pen to-morrow if you really want to do it (Hear, Hear). If you do that, the enemy will detect no lack of unity of purpose. It is possible to make it appear that there is no lack of unity of purpose.—Is it not a hundred times more desirable that there should be real unity of purpose?

IF THE KAISER CAME TO CALCUTTA?

"If the Kaiser came to Calcutta what would all the talk of freedom of individual, of the liberty of the subject, of the right of this people or that people to self-determination, of this constitutional reform or that constitutional reforms—what would be the value of all such talk if the Kaiser came to Calcutta ?"

Again, I say, we are in complete agreement with His Excellency, the Governor of Bengal. I believe, if the Kaiser came to this country to-morrow there would be no talk of liberty of the subject, of the right of freedom of the individual and of constitutional rights and that is the very reason why I am personally interested in not letting the Kaiser come to Calcutta (Laughter) and that is the very reason why we have been asking the Government again and again, why our leaders have asked the Government repeatedly, to do away with these repressive measures to call forth loyalty, not lip-loyalty but real and genuine loyalty—not loyalty to the Bureaucracy but to the Empire. You cannot call that up by sweet words alone, we want deeds —and as I say, this can be done by a stroke of the pen to-morrow if you really want to do it. (Hear, Hear and Laughter.)

MUST WE FEEL TO ORDER ?

His Excellency advanced another reason. It is this :—

" The British people have a temper of their own. Some people call them a stubborn and a stiff-necked race. They are, I belive, a fair and a just people. You can without difficulty reason with them, you can without difficulty excite their intrest, excite their sympathy and above all, you can excite their gratitude. But they are people, believe me, who resent, perhaps more deeply than any other people on this earth any suspicion that anybody is bent upon making an attempt to take advantage of them when their backs are against the wall."

Therefore, gentlemen, what does it come to? We must consider that wicked capacity of the German people who are for ever on their watch to find out a flaw in the constitution of this country. You must also regard the temperament of the British nation, who will be angry if you want your rights at this juncture, but the only people whose interests and whoso sentiments are to be set at naught are the Indian people (Shame). We are not men! We are not a race! Our feeling need not be considered—our sentiments are nothing! Our feelings must be those of our masters. We must feel to order and suppress our real feelings! (Shame).

NOT OBEDIENCE TO THE BUREAUCRACY BUT LOYALTY TO THE EMPIRE.

Well, gentlemen, I must say that I have read this part of His Excellency's speech with considerable pain. It is the duty of the Government, here, to consult and to consider the sentiments of the people. The people of this country are loyal to the Empire. They may not like the bureaucracy and they do not. And the British Cabinet has declared that the people are not wrong when they say that the

Bureaucracy has mismanaged matters. They do not like the Bureaucracy, and for sufficient reasons; but they are loyal to the Empire. Again, my earnest appeal to the Government is: "Take care, do not disregard the people's sentiments. Do not wish to substitute obedience to the Bureaucracy in place of the people's loyalty to the Empire. The people of this country are impatient and they will not bear it."

"For God's sake let this be the last chapter in the story of the great denial." (Loud Cheers).

ADVICE TO STUDENTS.

There was a huge meeting of students of Bangabashi and Ripon colleges on the 14th January 1921, at Mirzapur Park, when Mr. Das said :

Srijut Chittaranjan Das, who, on rising to speak, was given a very hearty ovation said "I am unable to deliver any speech to-day. My heart is full, and my voice is choked and I have not power and strength enough to express the feelings that are surging in my mind to-day. God has not given me power to express in language the happiness that you have given me by coming out of your Colleges. I feel it in my heart of hearts that, those of you who have come out, are greater than any of us here, and I humbly bow to you—to the manifestation of strength that you have displayed to-day. I want you to realise that,—to realise the strength in you. It is not yours—it is not human, it is the will—the divine will of the country and the God of our being. It is the will of *Deshamabrika* that has been manifested through you. What, she is, I do not know, but she is the Goddess of our Nation. I now can say with head, erect—blessed be thy waters, Mother Bengal, blessed be thy trees—blessed be thy sons.

I know people will call you mad. People call me mad too. But who are mad really? Are not the merchants and traders who are running after wealth and rolling in luxury—the lawyers and their clients who spend their all and are ruined by litigation—is it not they who are really mad? Whatever people may call you—you have got to realise the truth that is in you. Do stand upon that and stick to it, whatever difficulties may come or whatever sufferings may await you in the path. Dark and difficult are the ways, but Divine Light will guide you. Give up all weakness of the heart. Man can do everything. Remember we are men determined to emancipate our Motherland from bondage. Should we not be able to deliver her from the shackles that bind her?

We shall rather go ignorant than be educated in those schools and colleges. We want to be educated according to our own standard of living, keeping harmony with our past culture and tradition. I do not know what Bolshevism is. We want to realise what is truth—what is eternal—what is in our blood—for the salvation of our country. I want that. I do not want Bolshevism—I do not want industrialism". In short, I do not want Europeanism. I want to be a free man, and be myself again. If that is turth, depending upon that truth, fear not.

Another word, and I have done. I promise before you all, to-day, that, within fifteen days or utmost a month, we shall have a College—a National

College established, of which there is no equal here, and where you will get your national education, where you will learn to love your country and appreciate freedom. I want to see that edifice standing on the road-side of Goldighi pulled down brick by brick."

He concluded by saying that even the Medical Students also must come out. They would rather go, he said, without doctors than get the help of those who come out of that Institution aided by the Government.

Mr. Achyutaram of Bangabashi College said that he hailed from Andhra and they learnt all their national lessons at the feet of Bengal. When they saw that Bengal had not been doing anything they were getting disheartened. Now that Bengal was coming to herself again, he would be able to tell his fellow-countrymen in Andhra that things were all right in Bengal. Sriman Nagendranath Ghose said he was a student of Ripon College 1st year sec. B. When they were holding their meeting in the class about Non-Co-operation, a professor of the College remarked that the students were going to listen to the advice of "damned."—The students ought to strike for that if for nothing else.

The President, in bringing the proceedings to a close, said, that it had been already announced that a meeting would take place in College Square at 6 a.m. on Friday. A meeting would also be held at Mirzapur, Park, in the afternoon at 4-30 p.m. on the same day. He hoped that on the following day all students from the remaining colleges would come out. Medical Colleges and Engineering Colleges were not to be made exceptions in this matter. The Carmichael Medical College also should be emptied. If they could boycott the examination, the bankrupt University would come down in a day. When Post-Graduate and Law students were coming out, he felt convinced, that, no one would attend the convocation.

THE BATTLE OF FREEDOM.

APPEAL TO STUDENTS.

To-day I have to repeat the Message of Freedon. I have been often asked " what is the meaning of this movement." To my mind, the meaning is particularly clear. We want Freedom. We want to realise the right of regulating our own lives. We want to realise the right of building up the great Indian Nation. We want to compel the bureaucracy to recognise that right.

It is unnecessary to refer to the past. It is not my desire to perpetuate bitterness. It is my desire to strenghthen our determination to achieve our freedom.

I advocate the method of Non-Co-operation, as every other method has failed. I want you to cling to this method, come what may. This is our last chance and this, at least, will not be in vain.

Do you understand what Non-Co-operation means ? You must withdraw your help in moving the powerful machinery of the bureaucracy. Do you realise how you can move this machinery ? The bureaucracy works its wicked will through the pleaders, through doctors, through clerks, through their police officers and through Magistrates and Judges. And you now see what the Calcuta University contributes. It contributes all the strength upon which the strength of the bureaucracy depends.

I appeal to you to take away your hands from the wheel of this machinery. The first thing, therefore, is to come out of the Colleges. I make no distinction between the Medical students, between the students of the Engineering Colleges and other students. The problem is not of education, but of Non-co-operation. If you have this in view, how can there be any distinction between classes of students? Is it not clear that all students contribute to the strength of the bureaucracy? And is it possible to defeat this bureaucracy without taking away that help? I have heard arguments based on humanitarian ground; but every humanitarian ground must yield to the supreme necessity of the moment. There is some inconvenience, some apparent want of humanitarian consideration, in every great war. Is it possible that this great war, based on peaceful method as it is, should steer clear of all inconveniences? I do not believe that there will be any the more suffering, because of the withdrawal of medical students. I have given it my anxious thought, and my decision is clear. But even if it does involve great suffering, I should welcome that suffering, rather, than leave one stone in its place in the edifice of a monstrous Education. No, my dear friend, do not delude yourselves.

It is easy to quote Scripture to cover your weakness. Believe me, it is not the humanitarian ground which is keeping you away, but the imaginary prospects of worldly advancement which are dangled before your eyes. The method that I advocate is the method of sacrifice. If you have to destroy what you consider your chance of success in life, remember, it is only to defeat the bureaucracy, and to attain Swaraj. How can Swaraj be attained unless you realise your own right clearly, unhesitatingly? How can you compel the bureaucracy to recognise, that, which you yourself do not realise?

Do not listen to those who make careful calculations and tell you that this movement is bound to fail. I warn you against such doubts and hesitations. Even if the students do not realise their rights and their duty, the work of Non-co-operation will go on. But I admit that you may make it more difficult by refusing to join us.

The Battle of Freedom has never been won in the history of the world without sacrifice. The armed organizations of powerful bureaucracies, all over the world, have made armed resistance well nigh impossible. But the Soul is ever free, and he who is free in his mind can never be enslaved. I want you to turn away your face from Europe and from the organization which is of European character. I want you to concentrate your vision on the things which truly belong to us. The very simplicity of our life has become difficult of comprehension, because of the tortuous and complex organization which European culture and education have placed before us. Once you turn your face away from that, you will have faith in methods which belong to us in standards which are really part of our blood and of our bones. What is more simple than the desire and the determination to withdraw your help from that which is false and unrighteous? And yet why do you experience such difficulties in forming that desire and in fixing that determination? The answer is again the same, *viz.*, that Monster of education which is rearing up its head in defiance, as it were, of everything which belongs to us and which is dear to our hearts.

I repeat again—Wake up, wake up, wake up. We have slept too long. Realise the sense of your bondage and stand out boldly and firmly on the road to Freedom.—*The Servant.*

ADDRESS TO STUDENTS.

A monster public meeting was held at Mirzapur Square on 21st January, '21 after Mahatma Gandhi's address to the Students. Mr. C. R. Das, when asked to speak, was given a great ovation and said :—

Gentlemen, it is impossible for me, to-night, to make a speech to you, as my voice has not yet recovered. I desire to say only this—that there is but one duty before you at the present moment. Those of you who have left your Colleges do not go back or you bring discredit on the country, not only on Bengal but on the whole of India. Remember, the success of this movement is in your hands. I said that, the first day I addressed you, and that, I say to-night, again, that the success of this movement is in your hands. We want non-co-operation, we want all Government Institutions—educational or otherwise—should be boycotted. The question to-day is of educational institutions. Do not believe those who say that the Calcutta University is a National University or can even become the National University of Bengal. Avoid that reasoning because it is a false reasoning. The national character of an educational Institution does not lie in the fact as to whether the Professors are Indians or Europeans. The national character of the educational Institutions, to-day, depends on one fact, whether it is, or it is not, connected with the Bureaucratic Government of this country. That is the only test. They lead you astray. I speak with all the conviction there is in my heart, they lead you astray. Who say, that this College, Science College or that College or the other Colleges which are manned by Indians are National Institutions? They are not. They are Bureaucratic institutions and before we attain Swaraj this University, there, a few minutes walk from here, has got to come down. The youths of Bengal must make that perfectly clear. They have taken the first step. The second step is to continue in this boycott.

Then comes the question of National University. I told you the first day that, it is not necessary for Swaraj to have national Universities, but if you want them it is in your hand; and if you want them, and if you come out, I promise you a national University. I am here to make good that promise (hear, hear.) Nothing will deter me from fulfilling my promise. But, if you expect me to carry out my promise, may I not expect you to stand firm? (hear, hear). May I not expect you to be brave, to be true to yourselves and to shun those institutions you have set your face against?

Gentlemen, I am taking a list of two classes of

students of those who want to work for the country. The gospel of spinning wheel, which my revered leader Mahatma Gandhi has given you to-day, is a Gospel which India has heard before, but which, unfortunately for ourselves, India has forgotten, and it is not without pride that I am able to tell you to-day that, the curriculum which we were drawing up for the National University, makes the art of spinning and weaving a compulsory subject (hear, hear) for all students ; but those who want to work for the country must not only learn spinning and weaving, but they must also be trained in that particular work and it requires, at least, two months' training in the National University which I am anxious to build up on your behalf.

I have, also, made a second list of students who had told me that they want to continue their studies for whom I am providing or trying to provide. Always, remember, when I say I am doing this, I mean you are doing it. I told you the other day, my strength comes from your strength. I am nothing if you are not prepared. I have got the strength of a million men if you are ready.

What am I ? I am at your hands to-day for establishing this National University. But do not be under the impression that this university will be a replica of that monster of education which rears up its head over there. It is to be nothing like it; you will see that, when you study that curriculum which we are preparing, you must not expect luxuries. But I can assure that any student who studies in the National University for two years or even three years—I do not propose to have students in our institution for more than 3 or 4 or 5 years beginning from the age of eight or seven—and those who come out from our institutions, you will find, will be educated, will be recognizable as Indians, will be educated as Indians should be educated and will not be copyists of European maxims and European culture generally. That is the standard which I desire to apply, but be sure the work of education cannot stop; one year is nothing in the history of a nation—one year at a time when we are at war, peaceful though that war may be, when we are aspiring to the greatest, with the most powerful bureaucracy in the world—one year is nothing at all in point of time: and can anybody reasonably say that if you shun your books for that one year and take up this battle of Swaraj, you are not doing your duty? May I suggest that those of you who want to continue your studies will not be doing your duty in the battle of Swaraj? But those of you who are in the second, act in a manner true to yourselves, but whatever you do, remember that it is a non-violent war (hear, hear) Remember that if you go back to those colleges, after leaving them, you prove yourselves cowards and unworthy of being engaged in this great and glorious war.

Gentlemen, allow me, again, to thank you on behalf of my revered leader and my great friend Mr. Mahammad Ali (cries of "Bande Mataram.")

NON-CO-OPERATION

Mr. C. R. Das, in moving the Non-co-operation resolution at the Indian National Congress, Nagapur, 1920, said:—

I rise to move the resolution on Non-co-operation. I shall presently read the resolution before you; but before I do that, I ask you to consider it very carefully, word by word, and line by line, because I must emphatically deny the charge that the Non-co-operation resolution which was passed in the Subjects Committee, is weaker, and not stronger, than the resolution, which was passed in Calcutta. Let me first read this resolution. (Reads resolution). Gentlemen, let me put before you in a few words the scheme of it. We say that our wrongs, including the Khilafat, and the Punjab wrongs—I do not enumerate the wrongs because they are so many—that each wrong, so far as I am concerned, is a cause of the attitude that I have taken up. We declare that our wrongs are of such a nature that we must attain Swaraj immediately (hear, hear). Then, we declare that all other methods, which we have employed up to now, have failed and that, the only method which is left for us, is, the method.

of non-violent non-co-operation (hear, hear); and we declare that there must not be any mistake about it that this Congress has resolved definitely, clearly and without any ambiguity, that the whole of this scheme of non-co-operation shall be put in force to secure our rights and to attain Swaraj; and we declare further that, in the meantime, those things which we resolved upon at Calcutta, are to continue but not only those things, we are to direct our activities in other directions as well. Here I pause for a moment to consider the question which, I regret, has been raised, namely, that this resolution is weaker than the Calcutta resolution. May I ask you to consider in what respect is it weaker? I claim it is stronger it is fuller, it is more complete. In the Calcutta resolution, there was no clear declaration that this National Congress has resolved to put in force the entire scheme of non-co-operation down to the non-payment of taxes although I believe with Mahatma Gandhi that that may not be necessary. But still if that is necessary I want it to be clearly stated that the people of India will not shirk from putting that into force. Then we say that, in the meantime, till that call is sounded—and you must remember,gentlemen, directly the call is sounded, that call has to be obeyed by all sections of the community, lawyers, students, trades-men, merchants, agriculturists, every body, every section in the country must respond to that call (hear, hear) and do you understand what that means. That means that this tyrranical machinery of the Government is regulated—is driven, not regulated—by whom, not by the Bureaucracy but by the Indians; and it means that the moment that call is sounded, every Indian is to take his hands off that machinery (hear, hear) and compel this Government to do what you like. But ours are not the hands which will move your machinery (hear, hear). That is putting in force the entire scheme. Then, let us consider what we have got to do in the meantime. The Calcutta resolution was confined to the students and lawyers and a general resolution about boycott of foreign goods. Here we say we keep the same injunction with regard to students but we differentiate between students under 16 and students above 16. Then, with regard to lawyers, we keep not only the same thing, we re-affirm the Calcutta resolution, but we say that we are not satisfied with the way in which that resolution has heen responded to by lawyers; and we say that greater effort must be made to secure that; and also we refer to the scheme of settlement of disputes by private arbitration. Then comes the economic question, and we say that the economic drainage is one of the greatest wrongs from which we have suffered : and we say that a Committee of experts must be appointed at once to form and organise a plan of boycott of foreign goods. Then we come to the other question. We come to the boycott of Councils. We say that it has succeeded, and we say further what naturally follows from that, namely, that the men who are at present occupying those seats are not representatives of the people of India (Hear, Hear). Not only do we stop there, but we go further, that those people who pretend to represent them do not represent them, and therefore we call upon the voters not to take any political assistance from those people. And then we appeal generally, for unity in favour of the depressed classes, in favour of every section of the community which require protection and development more than we do. This is the scheme of the resolution. In what respect is it weaker? In respect of lawyers? I say 'no,' because it re-affirms but it continues to call upon lawyers to act up to that resolution. Is it weaker in any point? From the point of view of students, I say 'no.' I have guarded against students coming out under false sentiment. I think that it is right, that this greatest national assembly in India should declare that those students who feel the call of duty and conscience should immediately come out, regardless of consequence (Hear, hear). Is it weaker in respect of the boys under 16 years? I say what is weakness, and what is strength? We make it stronger by making it more just and more practical. Is it weaker in respect of the economic. question? I do not admit that, because in the general resolution which you had and which Mahatma Gandhi himself was to carry out, we have got a systematic plan of economic boycott and a practical boycott—a boycott which will not only be spoken of but acted upon by every Indian worth the name. I ask again,—where lies the weakness of such a resolution? It is nothing but the result of undue suspicion. I am making no appeal. I am making no personal appeal in my favour; but I do ask you to remember that when I say anything I mean it, and in my life on public questions I have never said anything which I do not believe in. Some of you may suspect, but all I can say, brother, ask me any question and I will answer, ask me what I intend to do, I will answer. Beyond that I will not refer to personal questions. I call upon you, in the name of all that is holy, to carry this resolution without one single dissentient voice. I want you to declare it to the nation and to the bureaucracy, and to the nation to realise their God-given rights. The rights exist, but rights have got to be realised. The rights exist because this is the eternal law of life ; but still every man and woman and every nation on earth has got to realise those rights. Realise the fact that we have got those rights and the moment you realise that the bureaucracy or any cracies in the world cannot stand against you and I want you to tell the bureaucracy that we have made up our minds to realise it, and we have made up our minds to compel you to recognise that which we have got. May God grant us strength not only to pass this resolution but to work upon this resolution and to carry out the great idea of which this resolution is the expression (loud cheers).

NON-CO-OPERATION

A very largely attended meeting was held in Maulana Mazhar-ul-Haqu's Compound on Friday, the 11th February 1921 at Patna when Mr. C. R. Das addressed as follows :—

My Friends, I must confess that it is somewhat difficult for me to address you on a subject on which I have been talking for the last, I don't know how many days. I am somewhat tired of making speeches. When I came to Bankipore I thought I would simply listen to speeches and that I shall have no trouble to address you. But I was prevailed upon to address you. I have been reading several newspapers lately just to understand the criticism against the policy of Non-co-operation. I read speeches of public men and of Government, non-officials, and of Governors. So I thought it might be hardly necessary for you to deal with those things but it might be useful to clear the grounds of principle and policy of the congress. I want to speak to you about the principle of Nationalism. We have heard the word Swaraj so much that we probably do not realise its full meaning. The principle of Nationalism is also the principle of

Swaraj. Swaraj is a convenient expression for adopting a cause which would be of Nationalism. Long before this policy of non-co-operation was started by Mahatma Gandhi, in fact in the year 1917, I remember what I spoke from the Congress platform at Calcutta. You remember in those days there was a great deal of controversy as to what would be the precise scheme of self-government. Bombay spoke the one way and Bengal the other. There were many differences of opinion as to what scheme of self-government there should be. Then I said it is useless to discuss the policy; we want to govern our own country, namely to govern ourselves and regulate our own conduct and develop the nation in the light of our own experiences. I say we want to realise that cause of nationalism. The moment we realise that, the moment we realise the right that God has given us, that moment the bureaucracy will be crushed under feet. The criticism which has been levelled against the Congress is this, namely, that the Congress has not defined what Swaraj is. Many people at Calcutta have taken this objection. My answer to that is very simple. The very nature of Swaraj is such that it is impossible to define it. Swaraj is that which you realise in your heart to day. How can you then define what sort of Swaraj you will get. Realise your right, and the moment you realise that right, the moment what you realise will become fact. If you realise less right you will have less fulfilment, if you realise in complete and absolute right, Swaraj you are bound to get. You cannot define it. India wants that and the moment India realises that whole heartedly, I say that moment Swaraj is ours. I care not whether you have Parliamentary councils, whether legislative councils divided into so many compartments whether you have upper house and lower houses in order to govern the country. I want India to say in one voice that we will govern ourselves. That is the right we have. No Government can deprive us of that right. The moment you discover that, you will get Swaraj. Therefore, before you think what kind of self-government we should have I want to tell you that you should concentrate your mind, day in and day out over the attainment of Swaraj. My justification for that is nationalism. Do you understand what nationalism is? Many people, very genuine and inteligent people say that they would not have nationalism because it is antagonistic to humanity. They forget that in this God's creation there are various nations and that India today pleads for her own nationalism. Indian nationalism does not and cannot hurt humanity. I understand by humanity several races that are inhabitants of this earth, Indians, Europeans, Americans, Russians, and others that are inhabitants of the globe and if I am pleading for nationalism of India to-day how I am going against humanity and nationalism of the earth. India's nationalism is according to her own traditions and principle, "Live and let live" according to your right. We have no quarrel with you but when you cut away our nationality and right, it is then we say that we will not co-operate with you. You develop your nation in your own way. You, Americans, you develop your nationalism in your own way. But if you say that Indian nationalism must be fashioned in your own way, killing our nationalism, that cannot be tolerated. Therefore you find nationalism and Swaraj to be absolutely the same thing. Here I give you an example. Take a garden. You see the beauty and glory of God's creation all round the garden. But if a flower says to another flower that it should not grow in its own way, is that possible? I say that so far as the law of hidden nature is concerned it should go in its own way. Each has got its own individuality, own nationality. This nation has got an absolutely distinct individuality. Is this nation to live according to European ideals? Do you think that an Indian can live according to English traditions? Indian nation must grow according to its own temperament in the light I have described. We have been trying to build our own nation for the last 35 years, but we have discovered to day that throughout the history of British rule every attempt made for the development of nationality was crushed by the bureaucracy. Wherever you strive for freedom there is every obstacle from the officials. Therefore what happened in the Punjab became possible. There was a Rowlat Act. It was to kill your nationalism and for that whole of India protested. No Nationality can prosper which has got a Government by bureaucracy of that character. Whatever you do they will come and check you, and ruin that line for ever. Therefore it is that the Congress has declared that every method which we had hitherto applied has failed. At the Amritsar Congress Mahatma Gandhi was for co-operation. I must confess I did not agree with that proposal. He is a good-hearted gentleman.

He told me is it not better to follow faith while co-operation has given such large promises. He thought that bureaucracy would change its angle of vision. I said that we cannot do so. And few months passed that Mahatma Gandhi was convinced that I was right. Congress has declared now, having regard to what happened in the Punjab, what happened to our Mohamedan brothren, and the passings of many oppressive laws from time to time. Congress has declared with one voice, and all provinces have accepted this time unanimously that the only method which remains is that of non-co-operation. It has been explained over and over again. Many people have asked me about that. I found it easy to explain in Bengal. The other day I had to address a large assembly of labourers of a mill near Calcutta. I told them that you work at mills, you have seen machinery, well, who is it that who drives the machinery. Who is it that makes the machinery work and produce articles and manufacture things. It is not that Burra Saheb who sits in a chair lording over the whole business. It is you who move the machinery. So many bags of papers come out because you move the machinery. I told them that the huge Government is nothing but a machinery. Who drives that machinery? It is ourselves. It is the students who read in colleges, it is the pleaders who practice in courts, it is the police officers, it is the Deputy Magistrates who decide cases, it is the judges who administer laws. So in every way it is the Indian that drives this machinery. A history of last 160 years shows explicitly that your objects are not our objects. Our object is to foster our development, your object is to crush our manhood. Therefore there is a complete difference between the object of bureaucracy and ours. Think what happened in Punjab and I cannot forget Khilafat either. These instances you cannot forget. You remember there was a non-official committee appointed by the Congress. Last year we all met at Benares and we signed the joint report as non-official commissioners. The report was drafted by Mahatma Gandhi. We examined that report and we discussed the matter. We purposely put our demands very low. In fact we put it so low that some of our countrymen were very angry. They asked much more than that. And now I tell you, it is no more a secret. We had made up our minds that we would put forward our demand and it ought to be no more a pious resolution and we must insist upon the Government to act up to our recommendation.

Our legitimate demands were so low. Even these demands were treated with scorn and the offenders were left scot free. Subscriptions were raised for those villans. Ladies danced, I am informed, to collect money for the up-keep of those villanous offenders. We entered into a contract there in the holy city of Benares. It is for this blunder that Mahatma Gandhi has started this non-co-operation. His object is that their hands are polluted, therefore, whatever their institution, no self respecting Indian can remain there. Every Indian should take his hands off from that Government. No Indian who has got any self-respect should go forward to help this bureaucracy. Mahatma Gandhi started it and after that my friend Mr. Moti Lall Nehru joined it. In Calcutta Congress I did not join it because there was great difference of opinion. Few read my speech because I was against non-co-operation at Calcutta. It is not a fact that I opposed that resolution on the very ground of non-co-operation. Once I have made up my mind to accept it, I must follow up to it. Afterwards I made up my mind that this Non-Co-operation must be more complete from the national point of view. I wanted to bring a more effective resolution. So far as my practice is concerned I have not accepted a single new case after the Calcutta Congress. I drafted another resolution. I specially went to Benares and there discussed the resolution with Mahatma Gandhi, with my friend Madan Mohan Malaviya, with my friend Lala

Lajpat Rai, I met again Mahatma Gandhi at Dacca and discussed with him again and he agreed to it. Those who knew of the inner working of Nagpur Congress might have known how I worked from morning till night for that resolution and I tell you I succeeded. It made clear that Non-Co-operation is that everybody should take his hands away from the machinery of Government and that until the whole country is not prepared for that we must go on stage by stage. That resolution is fully satisfactory. Mr. Jayakar of Bombay opposed it. He did not join us before. I do not know why. But I am glad to say that only the other day he declared that he has given up his practice as a lawyer and has become a non-co-operator. Therefore, every one who met at Benares and took that vow in the holy city of Benares have become non-co-operators. I have arrived at the conclusion that this life is not worth living and I would rather much sooner die than lead a life of a slave in this country. This country is ours given by God. We have to realise that day and night. I say again that the moment you realise that right that very moment Swaraj is ours. What is Swaraj? It is a right to carry on your own right in your own way. There is another thing before I have done. Mahatma Gandhiji's Charkha has caused much laughter before the officials. People who are saying so are totally ignorant of our slavery. Our slavery is more economic than political.

* * *

I was telling you something about Charkha. I have been asked in several places as to how Charkha could improve matters. How could Charkha bring Swaraj. Do you know what the facts are. Swaraj means that we must live within ourselves. We must be self-contained. I tell you that we are great slaves to-day. Our economic slavery is greater than political slavery. Exploitation is carried on by the bureaucracy. The Non-officials and officials so far as Europeans are concerned constitute the bureaucracy. One helps the other, so exploitation and administration are the two chief policies of the Government. I say our economic slavery is very great indeed and constitute the main factor of our dependence. The facts at present are that if Manchester and Lancashire stop sending cloth our women will have to go naked. That was not the case in India before this bureaucracy came here. Our system was not this. I speak of Bengal because I claim to know more about Bengal. The system obtained in India was, that so far as our necessaries were concerned we were self-contained. We never depended on any body in India. We made our own clothes and were independent of any race in the world. Now just consider what Charkha can do for you. From Manchester comes 60 crores of rupees worth of cloth every year. You will not have to pay these 60 crores of rupees which go out of India. If a householder works by Charkha for one or two hours a day at the end of the year he will find himself with all the necessaries of his family. For a clerk who gets 40 or 50 rupees per month, and who weaves his own cloth every day, it is a great deal of saving for him. It is very easy. One ordinary tree will yield one to 3 seers of cotton, And ¼th of a seer is quite enough for one Dhoti. If you use Charkha only for limited hours daily you will get sufficient cloth for a Dhoti. This Dhoti that I am wearing to-day will last 4 times longer than that which comes from Manchester. I tell you, you will solve it very easily. If the work is carried on all this year by every student and every householder, we will see the economic independence of India to-day. Along with it you will achieve your political independence. It is only for one year that we are asking for Charkha and after that you can regulate your methods. You do not want any mills. It is only for one year. Many ask, what about ship-building, what about navy etc., I say for God's sake, I do not want any thing for one year. If you once secure economic independence, I venture to say that India's economic development cannot be prevented by any power in the world. It will grow better and better every year. I know there is a great deal of discussion about it and personally I can tell you that I cannot for one moment be in favour of European industrialism at all. I shall not at all be sorry if some of the things that are manufactured in England are not made here. Do what you should do, work a Charkha and you will realise the result. If you do that you will without doubt get independence. Now, gentlemen, one word more and I have done. I have told you that non-co-operation is the only method to achieve freedom. I have also told you that the work of non-co-operation is very difficult. It will be destroyed if it is not kept by non-violent, method. The whole work will be impeded if it is not carried on non-violently. Every kind of violence mental or physical is detrimental to the method of non-co-operation. Therefore every non-co-operator's work must be strictly non-violent. He has to face danger after danger. Every non-co-operator will be inculcated, beaten, outraged but he should strictly maintain non-violence. You know the ways and methods of bureaucracy in this country. They have got so many sections in their Penal Code which they can use against any preacher of non-co-operation. I do not for one moment, think that these methods can ever root out non-co-operation. They know that the moment non-co-operation succeeds that very moment bureaucracy will be crushed. I know they will try to destroy the method of non-co-operation by using their penal sections. They may go on using section after section. But a non-co-operator should never indulge in violence.

Continuing Mr. Das said that he knew that proceedings have been started against certain workers in the district of Muzaffurpur under sections 107 and 144 of the C. P. C. for delivering violent speeches. They should not give any excuse like that to the bureaucracy. But now that they have been served with the notices they must comply with the section. Let the action of the bureaucracy be as autocratic, as autocrat can be. Let them break the law, and not the non-co-operators. If they found that the authorities were using section after section unjustly without any justification then the congress would have to declare civil disobedience. Time would then arrive to break the law. But that moment had not arrived yet. Their mission was the mission of law-abiding citizens.

If violence is used you will go against the Indian National Congress and destroy this sacred method. You must know in your heart of hearts the secret of Swaraj and that you will gain only by Non-co-operation. The only feeling, the only intense desire which a Non-co-operator should cherish, his only prayer to God, should be for the achievement of Swaraj. Gentlemen, now I am tired. I wish our movement a success in the province of Bihar.